The Corrections Toolbox

Surviving Your Career in a
County Jail

Dedication

This book is dedicated to the Corrections professionals of the Mendocino County Sheriff's Office, who showed up today for each other and for our community. This extraordinary group sees, hears, and experiences the sum of our failures as a society. They do so for twelve hours at a time, four to five days in a week for years, sometimes decades.

Every day, correctional staff members in your local jail face deep trauma from the inmates in their charge and care. These noble men and women offer some humanity to our communities' cast-aways and often provide the only positive human contact a forgotten person will receive. Guardians by nature and warriors, when necessary, Corrections professionals possess high levels of resiliency, kindness, patience and humor.

CONTENTS

ALL ABOVE CONTENT FIRST APPEARED IN CORRECTIONS1.COM

This wasn't part of the plan

I have not met one man or woman who wanted to be in jail when they grew up. If you ask any incarcerated adult on the planet today, none of them will tell you they had hopes and dreams of building muscles with push-ups in the yard at San Quentin State Prison by their mid-20s. The same goes for Corrections professionals. I don't recall daydreaming about that one day that I would be handed a set of Folger Adam keys with a briefing to start my twelve-hour shift at the Mendocino County Jail.

To be fair, Hollywood is not producing movies that celebrate the Corrections profession. "Corrections Deputy" is not on the top-ten dreamy jobs list.

Even after I started working in the Mendocino County Jail, in 2002, I had some serious questions about my life decisions and whether I was moving forward in the right direction. Ultimately, I applied for the job because I wanted a steady income. I had no idea what I was getting into. Looking back 20 years from the lens of a background investigator, I'm not sure I would have hired me back then. I just didn't fit the mold.

Two decades later, I also look back with pride that I stuck with it. I think back to the first group of people I worked with as a trainee. The unofficial leaders of the shift immediately found me a nickname and gave me grief by the heaping tablespoons, until I learned the job and got incrementally better at it. I have zero doubt that my success in Corrections was the direct result of a culture of excellence and high expectations from the men and women I depended on for my safety and mental wellbeing inside the walls of the Mendocino County Jail.

During my first week of orientation at the jail, I distinctly remember walking around with my Facility Training Officer and noticing he had more in common with the inmates at the jail than he did with me. I did not understand this dynamic until later in my career.

I see the "What am I doing here?" lightbulb go off for many applicants during the hiring process and I think every person who applies to work in Corrections should have an honest internal conversation before making a commitment to the profession.

When you consider this noble career, ask yourself if you are willing to work within a steel and concrete building for 48-60 hours a week. How much patience do you have for people who tell you every day it is their jobs to break your rules? Are you easily offended, or do you take verbal jabs personally? Can you get past your fears and walk into danger for your team? Do you have the internal fortitude to tell your partner when he is wrong? Will you thrive and remain positive while working in a negative environment, filled with failure? Without one accolade, will you make positive changes in your community?

Will you show up for your partners and take on your fair share of the work necessary to safely run a Corrections facility?

Maybe you shouldn't be a Corrections deputy

You don't have to look or act like a wrestling champion to work in Corrections. You will, however, need to possess a number of characteristics. Entering the hiring process to become a correctional deputy in California is much more involved than applying for a job at your local grocery store. Corrections deputy applicants must pass a written test, standardized by the State. Each applicant must pass an oral panel, where two to four interviewers score applicant answers to questions related to character and abilities.

Your reward for passing the written test and oral panel is the background process. You will be tasked with describing your life to date, answering uncomfortable questions about all your past challenges. You will come to terms with every mistake you have made in your lifetime, and each embarrassing moment you prefer not to talk about. Good news: no one is perfect, and your background investigator knows this. The investigator is more interested in your current perspective about the mistakes you have made and how much time and distance have passed between mistakes and the day you decided you wanted to be a peace officer.

More often than not, applicants who go into background to be corrections deputies end up disqualified from employment. The bottom line is that most people should not work in Corrections. It takes a combination of unique skills and character traits to survive the job. To survive the job for a few years without getting divorced, in trouble at work or generally jaded is even tougher. To *thrive* a couple or three decades in Corrections, you better know some things from the start. Keep reading.

Top character traits of a good candidate for Corrections

Many Corrections professionals are required to meet the same qualifications as sworn deputies on patrol. Included are minimum age and education requirements, and applicants must be free of felony convictions. Beyond the very black and white peace officer qualifications candidates must legally meet to move forward in the background process, there are patterns of behavior in every person which are useful in predicting how the individual will respond to working in a correctional facility.

Background Investigators interview family members, personal references, employment references, neighbors, property managers, housemates, ex-spouses and more to confirm a candidate's patterns of behavior meet job standards.

These are some of the patterns show character traits which may qualify or disqualify an applicant for the job.

Integrity:
The proclivity of an applicant to be honest, to do the right thing, for the right reason at the right time, is on its own the most important characteristic in a successful corrections deputy. Sheriff's offices and other law enforcement agencies depend on public trust to carry out their mandates effectively. Public trust is earned and maintained by being transparent and by owning our mistakes.

A background investigation will confirm that the applicant has earned and kept trust from the people in the applicant's life when it comes to matters of the truth, personal property, sensitive information and money. The applicant also must show she can carry out duties without demonstrating bias.

A Level Head:
How well can you regulate your emotions? Can you control your impulses? Corrections applicants must demonstrate they have a history of even-keel

behavior and have an overall "safety first" mindset. Success in Corrections means you can perform your duties well regardless of what is going on around you. When an inmate decides to fight with staff, controlling the threat without getting angry is a powerful tool baked into a successful corrections deputy.

Stress Tolerance / Resiliency:
Everyone has a breaking point, a moment when built up layers of stress, or prolonged, sustained stress will cause a person to lose control of emotions or critical decision-making capabilities. Background investigators search for evidence that Corrections candidates have a high threshold for stress tolerance and the tools to lower and minimize stress. Successful staff will also know when to ask for help and unpack trauma in a safe environment to stay healthy. Factors such as work/life balance play important roles in this area of investigation.

A candidate's past reactions to stressful situations help predict how she will respond to the Corrections environment. For example, a candidate who goes home to drink a six pack of beer after a stressful day will have less success than a candidate who takes stress out on a hiking trail, game of ball or time spent on a hobby.

The background investigation will focus on how often the applicant accepts his own short comings. Do you hide from your mistakes, or do you call yourself out when you screw up, shake it off, learn and move on? What's your recovery rate from making a mistake? Do you mope around for a day after breaking your favorite mug, or do you take a moment, laugh at yourself and give the mug a proper burial?

An investigator will want to know if you think you are a victim of life, or if you are the person who controls his own path and manifests his own success despite regular obstacles.

Emotional Intelligence:
A good Corrections candidate will demonstrate the ability to know when someone is being manipulative and how to effectively respond to the manipulation.

This is worth covering and will be repeated throughout this book. Corrections deputies must constantly focus on responding to critical incidents while putting their feelings on hold. Inmates regularly act out in ways that can provoke an angry response from staff members. A good Corrections candidate will show a history of being calm and collected in chaotic situations and of not being easily provoked into anger by the actions of others.

Just as importantly, a strong Corrections professional can identify when his own feelings, whether positive or negative, are affecting his judgement. Inmates will make regular attempts to change the way you do your job with as much positive emotional manipulation as negative.

Interpersonal Abilities and Communication:
Corrections deputies spend over 90% of their time communicating with inmates and with each other while on duty. More successful Corrections staff can interact with the inmate population in a manner that keeps groups of inmates calm throughout a shift, even while the staff member is admonishing bad behavior.

An applicant for Corrections will need to demonstrate self-confidence and the ability to persuade others without always using draconian measures. The candidate will need to show she can understand why people behave a certain way and key in on motivations for changed behavior. She will also need to demonstrate the ability to play well with others. Critical work gets done in a jail with support from a team. Cohesion within a team produces a much safer facility.

Conscientiousness:
How much do you care about doing a good job, about showing up on time, or meeting deadlines? When you borrow someone's car, do you bring it back with a full tank of gas? When you fill out all the background information in your hire packet, is it

complete? Do you make sure your essays cover what they need to cover? Are you a driven person? Can I trust you with my wallet? Did you file your income taxes last year? Do you pay your rent on time? Do you own your mistakes?

All these things matter a great deal in Corrections and a background investigator will clue in on any patterns an applicant demonstrates that show poor levels of personal responsibility or accountability.

What are we getting into, here?

I remember the first time I walked into the Mendocino County Jail. All my adult life, the county jail had stood about 20 miles from where I grew up. I didn't think about that jail one time before I applied for a job with the Sheriff's Office. Now here I was, in the hiring process and about to work in this mysterious complex, with barbed-wired perimeter fences and a culture that was foreign to me.

I didn't have much contact with either inmates or Corrections staff in my life prior to applying to work at the jail. I took the tour on a recommendation by my background investigator, who was probably struggling to make a connection between what he saw when he looked at me and comparing me with the job description of a Corrections deputy.

The Main Jail of the Mendocino County Corrections facility is an old-style, linear jail, with modules instead of pods and bars instead of solid doors. Think of the oldest working prison in California, San Quentin, arguably the worst neighborhood in Marin County.

Main Jail at Mendocino County's "Low Gap Hotel" looks like a smaller version of West Block at San Quentin. You may have seen West Block in the video footage of legendary rock band, Metallica, playing music for San Quentin prison inmates in May of 2003. Ironically, the band included the classics, "Kill 'Em All" and "Ride the Lightning" while playing at the prison, which houses Death Row inmates.

What struck me when I first walked into the Mendocino County Jail, especially Main Jail, was how heavy and loud the doors were. A thick metal door slams against a reenforced metal frame in a concrete hall with nothing to soak in the sound. You will hear the high pitch of metal on metal combined with the low bass of the massive door slamming with an echo off blank hallway walls for good measure. The metal door-slam is jarring when you first hear it.

I was also focused on how confined everything was. I saw small spaces with short ceilings at the Main Jail. I watched inmates walk around in tight counterclockwise circles around the internal perimeters of their dayrooms. Some inmates walked with a little more swivel in their shoulders, others with an uncaring swagger and there was an occasional inmate who would just walk around without any obvious purpose, looking lost, scared, or completely out of place.

In the parking lot, after my tour, I stared back at the building I had just left. I'm pretty sure it was out loud that I asked myself, "What am I getting into?" Somehow, with the help of good facility training officers and I'm not sure exactly what level of internal fortitude, I made it past employment probation, past the first five years, and way past the level of discomfort I felt on that first tour of the jail. Today, my jail feels like home. I didn't survive, however, without learning some good lessons along the way and stretching my own limits.

I am proud to say that, while I matured in a unique way because of my career in Corrections, I believe my years spent working in a jail did not change who I am or the core of my belief system any more than just growing up would have. I attribute my mostly unharmed psyche to the lessons I learned along my career path, and I consider myself fortunate to have thus far survived a profession which has the potential to ruin a person.

If you are working in a jail right now, you will agree that the inside of a correctional facility is not like anything in this world.

The inside of a jail, from the view of the incarcerated people, seems to operate much like a high school during lunch break, mixed with some more serious laws, borrowed by the inmates from the Animal Kingdom. The rules of a correctional institution often clash with rules that the inmates make for one another. The codes amongst the inmate population play a constant tug of war with the peace officer's code of ethics.

Regardless of why you find yourself in a housing unit at a county jail, the reality you are walking through is nothing like life on the outside of the facility's walls. This is true for the inmates and it is true for Corrections staff.

There are multiple paths to failure in a Corrections career. Without proper training and preparation, a Corrections deputy has very little chance of surviving the job. Even with good training, we face precarious situations regularly. Corrections deputies walk into harm's way, physically, emotionally, and legally every time we walk into a housing unit or escort an arrestee from a patrol car to Intake.

Those of us who make it through a Corrections career to retirement often do so at the cost of personal relationships at home. The Corrections profession joins other sworn professionals with a higher-than-average divorce rate. Additionally, retirement actuaries have figured that most of us will not live long enough past our careers to enjoy the full potential of our golden years. Suicide rates are higher in Corrections professionals than the population average. This does not have to be a reality moving forward.

Let's get you through this career in one piece.

Most of the lessons in this book came from personal experience, my own and my partners'. I made a good number of mistakes working in a jail. Each mistake I made working with inmates for over 15 years came with a lesson. Within 15 years, you will have the honor of learning from some of your own significant mistakes.

The intention of this book is to give you a head start on those 15 years with some of the tools you can use to successfully navigate external and internal hazards you will face.

This is where Corrections is going

All correctional facilities share common attributes, but there are some major differences between county jails and state or federal prisons. Jails are administered by county sheriffs, constitutional officers, who are elected by and answer to the communities where their jails are located. Most of the inmates in a county jail come from the community in which that jail sits. The friends and families of inmates in county jails have much more access to facility administrators than those of a state prison. The community has much more influence on a county jail than it does on prisons.

State and federal prisons house inmates who were convicted of crimes committed hundreds of miles, if not a state or two away from the correctional facility. Prison inmates will generally not return to the community in which a prison sits. Their sentences are overall longer than those of jail inmates, and correctional staff in prisons have less of an opportunity to affect the cultural atmosphere in prisons than the deputies do at a county jail.

This book is focused on the correctional setting in a county jail, as opposed to the setting in a state or federal prison.

Every corrections deputy working today is riding a wave of change that is coming from our communities, from within the justice system and from the Legislature. The wave already started years ago and will continue for some time.

Change is coming your way, whether you agree to ride the wave, or drown in its wake.

You will need to sharpen the skills you already have and be able to identify how you will meet new and increasingly difficult challenges you face in our county jail. You will be further challenged from inmates' family members, their attorneys and from advocates for police reform in your community. The silver lining to this wave is that you stand to get through your profession in much better shape than previously expected.

You may be reading this book as a new corrections deputy. You will learn at least one important lesson from this book that will strengthen your success rate, but only if you put the important lesson into practice and turn it into a habit. The lessons we learn in Corrections sometimes take a little bit of time and reflection before they make an impact on us. Some deputies come into this profession with a better set of skills than others. Some of us must learn a lot more in order to deal with the daily reality inside a jail.

As your career progresses, you will get wise to inmate games and learn how to talk to the most hostile crowd you've ever met. You will harden to survive emotional manipulations and some dark incidents without bringing that stuff home to your family. You will develop a darker sense of humor and the observational skills to know when you're walking by a parolee at the grocery store. As I said, however, the knowledge you gain while working in a jail is not without side effects.

You will need a companion skillset in order to come out of your experiences in good emotional health. There is a whole group of skills you learn to deal with in your day-to-day functions at the county jail. You will still, however, need to take care of yourself in order to keep coming back for extended shifts and go home smiling on the other side.

Your career will include perishable skills training, such as defensive tactics, First Aid, Contraband Searches, Cell Extractions and Legal Updates that guide a correctional institution's response to all the poor behaviors which inmates exhibit. This book is not focused on the basics you will learn and maintain with your training officers and instructors. This book is not focused on the laws governing county jails, that is best left to your Sheriff's lawyers and professional policy makers such as Lexipol.

What you will take away from this book is a set of tools which will help you manage an inmate population in a meaningful way, without causing yourself psychological damage or ruining your career. You will learn subtle ways to improve your performance and that of your institution. The lessons in this book will remind you of some perishable skills we all can easily lose over time, as we settle into a career in Corrections, the skills for which you were most likely hired. Most import, this book will help you survive and thrive in your career as a Corrections deputy.

Most of the content you are about to read is based on articles first published in Corrections1.com. The book can be read in pieces, starting with any chapter that gets your attention.

Thank you for your interest in the noble profession of Corrections!

"Whoever fights monsters should see to it that in the process he does not become a monster. And if you gaze long enough into an abyss, the abyss will gaze back into you."

- Friedrich Nietzsche

If you take nothing more from this book than the following sentence, I will have made a small difference in your career.

The inmates incarcerated in a county jail will ultimately return to the community.

This means if you live in the county you work in, I'm talking about your community that your inmates will return to. If you live in a different county than the one you work in, there is a jail in your county from which inmates will one day return to your community.

Most of the inmates released from your jail will also return to your jail. Why does this matter? It matters because these inmates, their friends and their families make up a portion of a community, for better or for worst. You have an incredible opportunity, one of the most significant opportunities, to improve your community just a little at a time with your tradecraft at the county jail. Proceed!

"Meh, so what? These people are not in my circle, I generally don't see them off duty. I don't even know they exist unless they are coming back to the jail. Plus, they do this stuff to themselves." These are all common and fair thoughts. Why take on this extra burden? It's not part of the job.

Directly, the lives of these inmates may not intersect with yours much. They definitely do intersect when the inmates come to your jail. Dealing with inmate behavior is part of the job, but you can have a direct hand in mitigating the volume of inmate behavior you will have to deal with in any given hour at the jail. Outside the jail, however, probably very rarely do we have contact with inmates, except in less populated communities.

Keep in mind, however, an inmate who returns to the community and continues committing crimes will cost your neighbors in stolen goods, destroyed property and, in the worst cases, violence. These are normally just statistics, but they affect everything from your home's value to the quality of life your kids will have at local parks. What's more is the people committing crimes in your community will have children, who may end up in your child's school or little league team. You will be affected by the inmates who return to your community.

I knew a local inmate for no less than a decade. He stayed in custody more than he stayed out. I would see him in the community – getting his next fix, stealing at the local grocery stores, finding a bridge to sleep under. At some point, I threw him away in my mind. To me, this man was a failure to himself. He was a failure to his family.

The discard

This man was also failed by the justice system to some degree. Maybe we were too harsh, not offering enough opportunities to escape the endless cycle of incarceration. Maybe we were too kind, with welcoming arms, fresh bedding and a warm meal at the jail. I discarded him as headed for certain death at a young age and a life less lived.

One day he was gone. Another face I wouldn't have to book again and again into the county jail. Maybe he was arrested in another county and started a new incarceration cycle on someone else's dime. Maybe he died. The unfortunate response to news of any jail regular's death is too often, "He's time served."

There were plenty more like him to fill the small void he left behind, new faces, soon to become regulars. I forgot about him and the jail continued on as if he had never existed.

There's a superstition in jails that you don't mention inmates who are out of custody. You shouldn't say, "Hey, I wonder what Joe Inmate is up to, we haven't seen him come in for months." This is like using the "Q" word. If you do, they'll come in just days after you've conjured them up. In essence, these people were doubly discarded.

I saw the man, about a year after I lost track of him. I was at a local store. I heard my last name called. Normally, this would be a coworker or an inmate. I turned to see **the discard**. He was wearing an apron and a big smile. He was working at the store.

The man came up to me, sheepishly at first. He wanted to extend an arm, but I saw him struggling with the unwritten rule that inmates and Corrections staff shouldn't have contact outside the jail. The rule comes from both sides. On the Inmate side, you're not supposed to be friendly with cops. On the Corrections side, we feel protective of our private lives, especially when our families are with us.

I extended my arm, and we shook hands.

I asked the man how he was doing. He told me he was so happy. He told me he was clean. He looked clean. He was thrilled to have a job, to be part of a team. He was thrilled to have relevance. I see him regularly now, and he always asks me how the jail is doing. I tell him it's full beyond capacity and we just don't have any room for him. He assures me he won't be visiting any time soon.

Statistically, this man stands a better chance of returning to jail than staying out. He functions well in the correctional setting; he even excels in it. He belongs to a social structure within the jail. The man can experience small successes while incarcerated and feel a sense of accomplishment from time to time, albeit a limited accomplishment that is downgraded by the stigma of being discarded by society.

Seek out good news

The Corrections world is filled with disappointment, sad stories and repeated failures. Corrections deputies and officers witness the repository of our society's misery refilled over and over in our facilities. It is imperative to our own well-being that we look for small wins inside the jail and in the community.

There is the habitual drunk whose birthday and social security number you've memorized because you've booked him in countless times. When he stays for a longer jail sentence, sobers up and gets his head clear, make contact with him. Tell him it's good to see him doing well.

When the inmate who's been on Administrative Segregation for half a year finally works her way down to General Population, tell that inmate it's good to see she made it out.

When you see the inmate kitchen worker hustling hard to get the place cleaned up, point him out and tell everyone listening it would be great to have someone like that working on the county roads. Make sure he hears you.

Corrections staff should actively seek out and identify good news coming from inmates. In celebrating the good news, you encourage more of it. You also broadcast loud and clear that you know an inmate is not automatically up to no good. You celebrate good news because it provides a counterweight, sometimes very small, to all the bad news.

Welcoming someone back to the community

The probability someone will return to jail should not stop the celebration of a successful stint out of jail. Corrections staff often avoid any interaction with past inmates, with good reason. We want to protect our families and ourselves.

Think for a moment what a positive interaction between a released inmate and you at the grocery store can accomplish. I would argue in most cases, a 30-second exchange with the ex-inmate creates a safer environment for your community and for your family. Most people want to fit into society in one way or another. Outcasts and discards are prompted to act out against the community by the very definition of the titles the community gives them.

In my own experience and that of other Corrections staff, this exact interaction has played out multiple times over the years. I walk down an aisle at the grocery store and run into Joe Smith, who is with his wife and his two kids. He sees me and smiles, "Hey Zaied! How's it going?"

"Hi Joe, I'm good. You?" I can call him by his first name because we're not in jail.

"Stayin' out of trouble. I've been clean for three months."

"Yeah, I've been staying out of trouble too," because Joe needs to understand I know staying out of trouble is a human condition we all live with, not just inmates.

"Well, I won't be seeing you in there anytime soon." Joe doesn't even want to say the word jail.

"Good, we're all filled up."

If Joe returns to the jail, his attitude towards me will most likely be respectful and cooperative. This helps create a safer environment in the jail. Joe's kids and his wife see the interaction and maybe their attitude towards Corrections staff is softened a little. This helps create a safer environment outside the jail. As well, if Joe returns to the jail, my attitude towards him is no less positive just because he has returned. I'm not the judge, I'm not the jury.

The balance

By building a rapport with inmates and engaging in positive interactions, Corrections staff can help create a more balanced environment in the jail. We see people at their worst. Sometimes, we see people when they are much better, even if just for small moments. These are victories.

Paying attention to victories in any size helps Corrections staff improve our own mental wellbeing as well. Seeking out good news fosters a more dynamic environment within a Corrections facility, an environment where behavior inside the facility is clearly more important than the simple fact that a person is incarcerated.

In the balance, a Corrections facility will find more cooperative inmates. The jail will be a safer place to work. It's also possible more people returning to the community, as society welcomes them back to be productive members, will stay in the community.

You've been on duty for seven hours with five more to go. It's your fifth 12-hour shift of the week and your patience meter is way down. Control directs you to the lobby to speak with a man about his son.

"Sir, how can I help you?" you ask. You start with a smile, but the words are routine. You're phoning it in at this point, but at least you're trying.

"Yeah, I hope you can help me," he replies. "The guy on the intercom couldn't help. I wanna know what's going on here! Can you please tell me what my son is doing in jail?"

This is public knowledge, and you tell the man why his son was arrested. You make every attempt to give the information he wants. You tell him why you cannot give him certain information. You deflect his veiled insults.

Finally, he says it,

"I pay your salary, you overpaid babysitter! You're not a cop. You're not even a man!" He finishes his barrage. His face is red. Your face is red too, and you want so badly to give him a piece of your mind.

How do you win when a tax-paying voter and a man not beholden to the strict behavioral rules set forth inside your jail directs his anger at you? How do you win an argument you lost on initial contact?

Turn it around

In incidents where a member of the public focuses verbal aggressions at Corrections staff, the most rewarding outcomes involve an apology on his or her part. Better yet, you get a "thank you" when all was said and done.

One obstacle in converting "screw you" to "thank you" is your ego. You're a correctional officer or a Corrections deputy. You may be a facility supervisor. You've had years of training. You know how to deescalate a violent mental health patient who may or may not know any better. You also know when it's "go time" and a flailing drunk has to be physically restrained. Most important, you know how to control a situation.

You can't, however, control a person in your lobby when that person hasn't broken any laws. You can excuse him. You can tell him you're done helping him because he's being rude. You can walk away.

Don't stop trying to help. Don't walk away.

A little empathy

The angry man who walked into your lobby isn't angry at you. He's probably not angry at the jail. Maybe he's not even angry with the officer who arrested his son. He's embarrassed. He's a little lost as to what to do. He doesn't have a clue how to navigate the justice system, or he's expecting the worst from past navigations. He's probably very angry at his son.

He wants you to be angry back at him and give him the satisfaction of honoring his poor expectations. He wants you to turn away so he can say, "You see! I told you these people are completely incompetent and what's more, they don't care!"

Engage the man. Address his anger, embarrassment and frustration.

"Man, we love our kids, don't we? They sure can give a man gray hair."

If you say that to any parent, I don't care how angry they are at the world, you will give that parent pause. You will make an instant connection. I've had people break down after I have said this, just moments after they charged into my lobby, ready to fight the world.

"They break our hearts sometimes, don't they?"

At this point, you are a dad and he is a dad. You've addressed, honored and validated what he is experiencing. Your conversation will be more cordial and your "no's" will land on softer ground.

Making "angry dad" acutely aware you care will open him up to tell you what he needs from you. None of his other needs will come close to breaking the barrier you've already torn down. He may want to know what the bail is – done! He may ask what's next – easy. He may want to know when his son goes to court. Tell him when. It's not a secret.

Build good will in your lobby

You've got plenty to do. Who has time to engage an angry man in the lobby? Inmates need to be fed. You're down two reports. You have a disciplinary hearing to follow up on. These functions are important, but don't discount the potential to build good will in the community. In a correctional setting, the lobby provides most your contact with the public. We build public trust one contact at a time in that lobby.

Imagine if you have 100 percent contact satisfaction when parents, lawyers, bail bonds agents and doctors walk away from your lobby, regardless of what condition each came into that lobby. What support will your jail receive if there's a false complaint of mistreatment? How will the community respond when the jail needs help, understanding or empathy?

Imagine the day you walk by the tattooed OG who only cares about his mother and sister. This guy cares little for the law or anyone outside his family and gang. You walk by him, and he stops you. He's got a serious look on his face, and you brace yourself for a complaint, or attempted demand. The inmate nods and thanks you for treating his family with respect when they came into your lobby last week. Who wins in this scenario?

Because it is who we serve

At the end of the day, most inmates come from social circles that include the people who will end up in your lobby. When we help our angry lobby dads, we improve the jail's standing with the citizenry. In doing so, we carry out our mission to serve and further partnerships in the community.

The majority of civilians have no idea what happens inside a correctional facility. Most of the American population enjoys total ignorance of the work environment correctional deputies face every day. That is, until an incident in a correctional facility ends up in the news.

What is often missing when these news stories are published is the context communities need to understand the whole picture of what led up to a reported incident and what steps were taken before, during and after the incident in order to keep staff, inmates and the surrounding community safe.

The new partnership paradigm

In today's socio-political environment there is an expectation of complete transparency from all law enforcement operations. With civilian review boards, audio and video recordings readily available to the community and deeper public information laws, it has become even more critical that incidents the public sees happening in correctional facilities are provided with the context of a bigger picture.

There are two groups within our communities who can provide a bridge between that important big picture of correctional facilities and the people which correctional institutions must answer to regularly.

The first group consists of the civilians who work daily alongside sworn staff. This group includes some of our best advocates when the community expresses concern about incidents in a jail. The civilians who work in jails see regular operations within those facilities and have the context with which to understand how sworn staff conduct their duties and why.

Civilians working within a jail or prison have traditionally been treated as outsiders to varying degrees. This practice has been a disservice to the Corrections field. It is more important than ever to bridge the gap between civilian and sworn staff in your jail. Your facility's civilian staff should be treated as partners, just as you treat fellow officers.

You support your partners to such a high degree on and off duty because of your shared experience. Why then would you not want members of your connected civilian staff to have that shared experience and, by extension, a more holistic perspective on the reality of Corrections? Our level of partnership with fellow officers needs to be extended beyond the uniforms we wear to the civilians who already work side by side with sworn staff.

Instead of seeing facility chaplains, nurses, educators, mental health care providers, and other civilians who have regular contact with your inmates as a nuisance, standing in the way of your duties, treat them as part of your team. Include civilian staff in appropriate trainings with sworn staff and include them when you gather information to make changes in the way you do business. Their understanding and empathy for your duties will be shared with friends and family, who may be more open to a civilian perspective.

There is a second group of civilians who can help bring a big-picture understanding of correctional facilities to our communities. This group is made up of community stakeholders, civilians trusted by other members of the community to advocate on behalf of the public. This group is generally made up of elected and appointed officials but should be made to include other interested parties.

In a Critical Incident Team training, held in 2019, a sheriff invited members of the local Grand Jury to the training. The members of the Grand Jury sat through the entire training and participated, along with many members of law enforcement, in the discourse that occurred within the training.

By the end of the training, the Grand Jury members had a much more accurate perspective on how Corrections staff respond to critical incidents, specifically involving mental health patients. This civilian panel also learned what was being done (through the training) to improve services to the community. During breaks and lunch, the members of the Grand Jury had opportunities, through frank discussions, to truly delve into the realities faced by correctional staff on the ground.

A new level of understanding

Why invite an untrained and inexperienced group of people to see in detail how Corrections staff members do their job day in and day out? Are we not opening up a conduit for potential criticism of our methods? I would argue that we are, but that this process could serve to improve our methods in Corrections and bring them in closer alignment with the communities we serve. It also dispels misunderstandings community members may have about how correctional facilities operate and open up new perspectives on what actually happens in jails.

Correctional facilities should safely and within the boundaries of confidentiality conduct regular tours in order to remove the curtain of mystery from these institutions. The tours are a good opportunity to answer questions and help the community understand the realities of our jails and prisons. Command staff should have regular dialogue with community stakeholders in order to share and address concerns.

Creating new partners in Corrections from the civilian world has great potential to add depth to a better level of understanding from our surrounding communities. These partnerships also serve to remove a high level of ignorance about Corrections within communities, spreading the responsibility beyond sworn staff of solving social issues tied to incarceration. These stronger partnerships should start with the civilian connections we already have in our jails and prisons and spread beyond our facility walls to the community.

Treat members of the civilian world as partners and, in time, you will find that your community, fortified with a healthy perspective about the realities of our institutional environment, will respond with empathy for the difficult job you do.

Running a correctional facility which is transparent to the community can improve public perspective about Corrections and give communities less room for wrongful interpretations when Corrections does end up in the news. In bringing a community closer to the correctional environment, we also create stronger partnerships in society, thereby spreading the responsibilities we are saddled with to our civilian partners and improving our expected level of service to the community.

Where is the help?

You are a housing deputy, running the floor. Commissary comes through after lunch. It's going to be tight. You will be focused for at least an hour, making sure the inmates get their care packages, chips, candy and shampoo. The nurse needs to see a laundry list of special housing inmates, maintenance still has to fix that main door into B-Mod, and your partner called in sick today.

You better hit the floor running and keep everything moving. Every hiccup and roadblock will be a challenge to your overriding mission of safety and security. This is a jail and if things don't go right, it's ultimately on you.

Any help from the booking deputies is non-existent today. Do they even know what you're dealing with today? Control seems to be running molasses slow. You find yourself standing at doors for too long. You are itching to call the operator out on your radio. You wonder, "What's taking so long?"

It's time to let a group of inmates out to use the day room, but Classification walks in to conduct an interview. The classification officer explains she's behind on this interview. It has to be done right now. You will have to let the group out later, maybe after lunch. The nurse shows up with the list. "How many can we get done before lunch?"

You're experiencing competing mission objective overload. In your eyes, at this moment, you are juggling the most pressing issues unfolding in the jail. Can't everyone see what you're up against? You ask yourself, "Where's the help? Who's paying attention? Why can't I get some assistance in here!?"

Your break comes and you're sent off for a few quiet moments. First stop? Control, to tell him he better start paying attention! You get up to the tower, loaded with demands and questions. The control board operator is breaking a sweat. It looks like he's playing the piano; bells are going off from every corner of the jail; Half his monitors have shut down and his phone is ringing. He looks at you with relief. "I need some help here…"

The horse race

We often work with blinders on, focused on our own set of tasks. Our perceived importance of those tasks is enhanced by our own connection to the outcomes. How many times have you become irritated with a fellow team member for failing to recognize how busy you are with an imperative mission? How many times have you failed to recognize a team member who is just as dedicated and focused on her own mission for that day? Take off the blinders.

The first step to becoming an effective member of any team is to consider the whole picture while you're contently pressing forward in your own part of the universe. I promise you will also start to think as a leader thinks. Big picture thinking will make you a better candidate for promotion.

Jump in!

Every Corrections facility, by its nature, involves a series of events and situations with varying levels of pressure and competing interests. Murphy's Law applies on a massive level and you sometimes don't know where and when the next emergency will unfold, just that it will.

At this moment, it will be a fight in your housing unit. In a half-hour, it will be a flood down the hall. Sometimes we need to reallocate ourselves to help address "someone else's" problem. After all, is any problem in your jail REALLY someone else's problem? **Jump in!**

I'll get that

My favorite words to hear on shift are, *"I'll get that."* This means a deputy is juggling tasks. A second deputy with blinders *off* observes the need for help. The second deputy actively changes course, and he jumps in. Does your jail have an "I'll get that" culture? If not, you can shift to a culture of team service that will pay dividends down the road.

Try it for one week. You'll have to be on your game. Focus on maintaining enough efficiency in your own work by avoiding unnecessary distractions and moving from one task to another with less break time in between those tasks. Make it your goal to set aside time for others. Don't expect anything in return. Just jump in when you see a need. Others will follow. Everyone had to test to get into this career field; we're a bright bunch.

From an outside observer's perspective, *including inmates*, a culture of teammates who instinctively jump in for each other is harder to divide and conquer. As you know, the most sophisticated inmates tend to play psychological games with staff. Have you ever heard an inmate make a grand proclamation that you're the hardest working deputy in the jail, then slip in that it seems you never get any help? The inmate is trying to separate you from the team and that inmate will fail in a healthy "I'll get that" culture.

What about "that guy"

What do you do with the team member who doesn't serve the team? Maybe you have someone on your team who sheepishly asks for help much more than offering it. He may suffer from chronic self-doubt, marginal motivation and regular browbeating. Most likely, everyone in your well-oiled machine has given up on him. Throw him a lifeline. Ask for help.

Helpers feel needed and important. The psychological benefits of giving and helping are well documented. The teammate who doesn't get it may just need to be reminded how good it feels to be needed. More importantly, that teammate is more vulnerable to inmate games while shunned by his teammates. Look for teammates who resist positive change and bring them back into the team.

Who serves whom?

Lets take the service concept one step further. Control and tower operators generally serve everyone else in the facility. How could a movement deputy serve the control operator? What can the nurse do to serve the smoother movement of inmates to the medical room?

The movement deputy can choose the most direct paths, when possible, while moving inmates. Anyone being served by the control operator should be aware of how many movements may be occurring at one time and be patient. The nurse can make inmate movement lists grouped by housing unit with updated and clearly listed housing assignments. A housing deputy can serve booking staff by filling out sobering cell observation logs on the way through Booking. The housing deputy is already there. 25 extra seconds, helping your team out will make a big difference.

Why is it so important to clearly mark down information on your paperwork? Because that clear information will serve someone down the line who has to read your paperwork. We write clear, concise and complete reports to better serve whoever needs to make information-based decisions tomorrow, next week or months down the road.

When you consider who your work could possibly affect one, two or three steps down the line, you become a better servant to your teammates. Even the most seemingly mundane tasks can take on more significance when we all stop to consider whom the tasks serve. We are in the service business. We succeed in serving the public. We do great in serving our mission. When was the last time you set aside your own set of tasks for just a moment to throw someone a lifeline.

When was the last time you served your team?

It is lunchtime at the county jail and Corrections Deputy Lambert has a crew of inmates serving meals at the front gate to D-Pod. Deputy Stark is bringing an especially difficult inmate, a mental health patient, back from court and into the housing unit. Stark needs Lambert to move his crew in order to return his inmate. Lambert tells Stark to wait with the inmate until he is finished serving lunch. Under his breath, Lambert says, "That dude (Stark) needs to learn it's not all about him." Inmates from the crew hear him.

While they wait to get into D-Pod, Stark's inmate becomes impatient and quickly gets hostile. Stark calls for backup and ends up having to subdue the inmate. Stark and his backup are eventually able to escort the inmate to a safety cell. Stark is angry. "It would have taken three minutes out of the lunch service to let me escort my guy into the unit," Stark complains to a fellow deputy as they walk past two inmates, mopping the hall floors.

The story grows legs and soon other deputies are pontificating on the matter, some taking Stark's position. Lambert definitely should have paused lunch service to move a difficult inmate back to the safety of a cell. Others side with Lambert. Meal service shouldn't be interrupted for movement. Stark should have held the inmate in the booking area until meals were finished.

For the remainder of the day, the tension between Stark and Lambert can be heard in their radio traffic back and forth and in their complaints to fellow deputies. Inmates hear some of the traffic and complaints and can see the tension between Stark and Lambert any time the two work in the same space.

Inmates are always watching you

Inmates can tell when staff members are not getting along. They watch how we interact, and they listen for tension in our radio traffic. Inmates observe us in the housing unit. They see how often staff members will join the floor officer and offer help, or when the floor officer is being ignored by the rest of the shift. Inmates take note when the floor officer responds to radio traffic with a shoulder shrug, a headshake or a frustrated sigh.

Inmates listen to everything Corrections deputies say. Some use information strategically in any way they can, whether it's extra yard time due to lack of staff communication, or a planned attack, knowing a shift doesn't work as a cohesive unit.

Knowing there is internal strife on a shift, inmates will often complain to you about the staff member you just relieved or will tell you how much better a job you're doing than your partner, who may be standing right next to you. Others will completely ignore a floor officer and ask questions of another officer who just walked in.

The odds are that an inmate is stroking your ego for a favor down the road. He may also be attempting to create division between you and another deputy. If the inmate has already observed staff infighting, the inmate could be looking for ways to increase the division between team members.

We are all on the same team

My good friend and mentor Rich Spurling told me, "Inmates outnumber staff 30 to 1, but we are the most organized (group) in this jail. That's how we stay safe."

Inmates should be under the impression that any shift working a facility is a tight, cohesive unit, with members willing to take reports for each other, back each other's plays and communicate constantly throughout the day. If your partner has a problem with the cleanliness of a cell, it should be your problem as well, regardless of what you think about the matter.

When you disagree with your partner, hash out your disagreements in the break room, far away from inmate eyes and ears. Don't ignore the slightest issues. Work them out, even if the subject matter is uncomfortable and you find it easier to just stay quiet. Until you work out any differences with fellow staff members, inmates will see an opportunity to cultivate division. Supervisors play a key role in pinpointing tension between staff members and addressing that tension quickly in a setting off the jail floor.

Complain up the chain

We all know complaints, hopefully with proposed solutions, should be made to a supervisor. Most likely, you have shared a complaint or two with your shift mates, maybe more than two. This basic rule should be applied tenfold with inmates. If you're complaining to an inmate, you better be complaining about the weather or road conditions.

If an inmate tries to fish complaints out of you, call her on it. Make statements to support your teammates and the chain of command. If you can't hide your disappointment with a new directive and the inmate manages to figure this out, use your final line of institutional solidarity. Tell the inmate it really doesn't matter what you think about the directive, the boss wants it so and the boss will get it as ordered. Period.

Legitimate grievances

Once in a while, an inmate will come to you with a genuine complaint about a staff member or you'll witness staff acting in a questionable manner toward an inmate. It's never a comfortable feeling to be anywhere near this type of situation, but it happens. You should know ahead of time what you'll do to protect your organization and, at the end of the day, your team, including the wrongdoer.

The specifics of handling bad peer behavior are a subject for another day. What you communicate to inmates when handling negative staff behavior is as important as addressing the behavior. While you don't want to present a broken team to inmates, you do want to communicate to inmates that they should expect a standard in how staff behaves in a correctional setting. Don't ignore mistakes you've made or witnessed. The philosophy of public trust for law enforcement extends to the inmate population.

If an inmate comes to you with a legitimate gripe about a fellow staff member, first separate out the behavior from the person being complained about. Advise the inmate that is not how the jail does business but be careful not to condemn your teammate. You don't know if the allegation is even real, just that the alleged behavior itself is bad business.

Advise the inmate of the grievance process. I like to do this even when an inmate accuses me of wrongdoing, as you are giving the inmate a vehicle to address his issue. When an inmate prods you to condemn a coworker for alleged bad behavior, remind him that while you think the described behavior is bad, you don't have the luxury of knowing what happened, because you were not there.

Inmates often accuse Corrections officers of protectionism when officers refuse to side with inmates against fellow staff members. Sometimes those accusations are another ploy to divide staff. Inmates don't need to know what process takes place behind the scenes to correct staff wrongs; only that as an institution, a prison or a jail will address staff mistakes.

The correctional team

Regardless of how we feel about fellow staff members, the appearance to inmates should be that the deputies minding a correctional facility work together as a well-oiled machine. Our intrapersonal issues should be a mystery to the inmate population. Regardless of what you think about a specific directive from the chain of command or your partner's priorities, your presentation needs to be that of support and buy-in. Even when we address bad staff behavior, we do so while presenting a united front for inmates. The presentation of a cohesive unit is a preemptive defense against any inmate manipulation to create and broaden divisions in the correctional team.

You come into briefing and the sergeant is handing out assignments. You have been running housing units for the past three days and your patience meter is a little low.

The sergeant points at you and says, "Take Control."

This will be a break from the trenches. You won't have any real inmate contact for the coming shift. Someone jabs you and asks if you're on light duty. You grab your backpack, loosen your keepers and head to Control to start your shift.

You get your briefing and settle in, getting ready to respond to calls for movement from housing deputies, nurses, lawyers in the lobby and the rest of your team. There are four arrestees pacing around in safety cells, four sleeping in the sobering cell and countless arrestees in holding cells, waiting to be processed from a busy Friday night.

Respond to calls wisely, even when you're busy

It doesn't take long for the first call to come in, an arrestee in a crowded holding cell. You listen to the list of demands and the familiar responses crop up in your mind as you take a look at the monitor to make sure the guy is not in need of life-saving measures. Meanwhile, two floor officers need to get into their housing unit, the nurse is ready to see her list of patients.

"Hey, I've been here for two hours already, why can't you guys tell me what's going on?!" (*Two hours? You're lucky. I don't even know your name buddy.*) "I want to call my lawyer, but no one is answering." (*It's Saturday, your lawyer is fishing.*) "When am I going to court?" (*Same schedule. Has been for decades now.*) "Why can't I go now?" (*First come, first served buddy. Maybe less drinking in public next time.*) "I need some toilet paper in here!!???" (*I haven't perfected teleportation, my friend. Can't help you there.*)

You could verbalize any of the above responses and maybe get a laugh out of the other arrestees in the holding cell. You'll get the guy on the other side of the intercom off your back. He may not bug you again and you can continue on with your duties. The arrestees in that holding cell will get the clear message you're not there to help them with their trivial needs. You will have set a sarcastic tone in that cell, which may carry over from the arrestees to the next staff member who contacts them.

The guy in holding will leave you alone, but his concerns, being very real to him at that moment, will keep him upset and his anger will fester. Eventually, he may be the guy in the holding cell who tears the phone off the wall or punches another arrestee. It won't be your report. Not your problem right?

Booking staff may have to tackle the angry arrestee and do what they can to safely move him to a padded cell. You won't have to write the crime report and testify in court about the broken phone or the guy who got punched and taken to the hospital. You probably won't have to be on the transport detail to the hospital. Your partners will handle everything. You're just opening doors and answering calls.

Make time to help your team

Control officers are often very busy focusing on keeping inmates in the right places within a jail or a prison, keeping staff safely on the move, and generally keeping an overall eye on the security of the facility. A control officer doesn't normally have much time to spare for chats. But we get little breaks in the action periodically. What if during those breaks we took the time to address a concern, or commiserate with an arrestee that it's just not fair those lawyers don't work on the weekends? "I mean, we're all here, right??"

When you run a control center, you have regular contact with many inmates in a large area of your facility, sometimes the entire facility. You often broadcast announcements to entire housing units. In your regular contacts with other staff members and with inmates, you have the ability to help affect the tone for that shift. You are as close as it gets to the morning disk jockey at a radio station, getting people through their commute.

When responding to inmates who initiate your intercoms, you can blow them off for non-emergency requests and agitate the inmates with sarcastic remarks, or you can choose to use calming responses, a caring tone and just a little bit of empathetic feedback. Remember, your response will not affect you much, but what you say and do when you are assigned to Control *will* affect your partners who are in contact with inmates all shift.

Small efforts pay big returns

When an inmate calls you from her cell, do you answer professionally, or do you say, "What do you want?" When you announce a lockdown in a housing unit, are you firm in your tone, or are you barking angry orders? If you know that Inmate Smith is calling, do you ever ask, "What's going on, Mr. Smith?" All these little details add up to setting a tone in your facility that influences behavior in inmates. Since the control officer is communicating with many inmates regularly, these details end up effecting the general safety of your entire facility.

The next time a mental health patient calls you from his Administration Segregation (Ad/Seg) cell and asks you what day it is, tell him what day it is. Tell him what it's like outside. Tell him you're going to try to check up on him later, and then check up on him later. This will take all of 15 seconds per contact. If you have other calls coming in, tell him you have to go, but say, "Have a good day, man." What you may be doing is reducing his stress level just a little with some brief, but much needed, positive human contact. Just as important, you will be reducing the possibility this inmate will go to his window and yell obscenities or bang on the window for hours, irritating other inmates and generally making your floor officer's job harder.

If an agitated arrestee contacts you from a holding cell with demands and questions, try to address some of his needs, and if you can't address the questions and demands, take the extra 20 seconds to let him know why you can't. Do this with empathy, even if he is angry and spiteful. Your response may or may not deescalate the arrestee. However, the other arrestees in the holding cell with him will hear you.

Choose to set a positive tone from Control

When you speak positively with an inmate in a group setting, remember you are broadcasting a level of care the other inmates will hear and you may reduce some of their anxiety, even when you are not speaking with them directly. When you rise above the anger and spite directed at you and you respond with professional calm, you are taking away the agitated inmate's reasons (however unreasonable) to intensify his behavior.

Imagine being the booking deputy who checks up on a cell full of arrestees after the arrestees have had positive contact with the control officer. The arrestees would be slightly less edgy because the tone of positive staff contact has already been set and can easily translate from one staff member to another. Control officers can easily create that positive tone with very little effort by just being mindful of how they speak when answering calls all shift.

You're walking through your assigned housing unit for an initial headcount. Someone yells out, "It's Deputy Jones, everyone be cool today!" That's right, they know not to mess with you. You won't put up with any guff. You're a hard charger, you get things done, and these guys respect you.

Later, during lunch service, one of the inmates gets an extra tray and walks away, pretending he can't hear you while you yell for him to come back. You're irritated. He got one over on you. The inmate tricked you in front of the entire housing unit. Some of the inmates are laughing. They can tell you are unhappy.

About an hour before shift change, you cover the Ad/Seg unit for one of your partners. One of the inmates you put in Ad/Seg just a week prior yells at you from behind his door.

"Hey Jones, you ain't nothing without that radio." The inmate is angry. "Why don't you take that badge off like a man and come in my cell. You're not so tough without all your little friends." Other inmates are standing at their door, watching you, waiting to see what you are going to do.

"Kick his ass, Jones," another inmate yells at you, encouragingly "I've seen you fight, bro, that guy just likes to flap his gums!" The inmate who first yelled at you starts mule kicking his cell door. You've had enough. It's been a long day. Inmates see that you're angry. This guy is disturbing the housing unit. If you don't deal with him now, other inmates will know this behavior won't go unchecked.

Some of the inmates are already banging on their cell doors. Others are encouraging you to open the mule-kicking inmate's cell door and "handle your business." You've lost control of the housing unit. You just want to call in the cavalry and drag his happy ass through the dayroom to show the other inmates this type of behavior will not be tolerated. This is your jail.

As you consider your quickly dwindling options, you look over at the mule-kicker's cell. Encouraged by the chaos and attention he has just created, he is now flooding his cell. You're going to be writing your report well past shift change. This could have turned out differently.

Remove your ego

Inmates rely on the ego of correctional staff for several reasons. They use your ego to manipulate you when they pay you complements. Inmates employ your ego for entertainment. Just seeing correctional staff lose control of their emotions gives inmates a sense of power and satisfaction. In more serious cases, inmates will use correctional staff members' egos to snare us into an incident that can end in termination or worse, a conviction for unnecessary use of force.

One of the best ways to bolster your resiliency throughout a career in Corrections is to remove your ego from the duties you carry out. Removing your ego takes your emotional response to inmate behavior out of the equation. Do not dwell on inmate behavior, regardless if it's meant to make you feel good or bad. Just deal with the behavior and move on.

When an inmate is behaving badly, he is not behaving badly for you specifically. He is just behaving badly. Period. Take yourself out of any thoughts about inmate behavior and you will understand that the inmate will behave the same way with or without you.

When you observe inmates misbehaving with other staff members, do you sometimes say to yourself, "Ha! If that was me in there, that behavior would not be going down the way it is with Jones." Maybe what you are telling yourself is true, but what you are doing is attaching your ego to inmate behavior.

This is just business

One place to start working on your ego in a correctional setting is in your response to the complements inmates pay you. Next time an inmate announces to other inmates not to mess with you, remind yourself that controlling a housing unit and correcting inmate behavior are your assigned duties, not some award-winning magic show you've been working on for the last decade.

When an inmate pulls an extra lunch tray from you, take note. Escort the inmate out of the housing unit, tell him, "That was pretty slick," hand him a rule violation, and move on. If you want to address the slick move right away, do it in the housing unit. Address the behavior with some humor, "thank you Inmate Smith for being part of the facility training program, I'll need you to sign your commendation (meaning, a rule violation) later on." Inmates will immediately turn their laughter on Inmate Smith for getting caught and written up.

However you respond, do not act with anger. Respond with clear non-verbal communication that this was a blip in your day and, most importantly, the behavior did not affect how you will behave during the rest of your shift.

Remove your ego to deescalate a hostile inmate

When an inmate challenges you to come into his cell and "be a man," there is not one ego-driven response that will end well for you. If you tell the threatening inmate he wouldn't last two seconds fighting you, you are now back in middle school, at recess, with a group of kids chanting, "Fight. Fight. Fight. Fight." The moment you let your ego make decisions for you, you have lost any interaction with an inmate.

There is absolutely no reason you need to prove your muster to any inmate who challenges you to a fight. If you really want to show the other inmates how your team can handle this window warrior, you might as well bring your pension into the cell and hand it to the inmate. He just won. Remove your ego when you address a hostile inmate.

When the inmate you put in Ad/Seg, challenges you to a fight from behind a locked door, address the behavior. Ask the inmate why he's so angry. Ask him if he understands why he's on lockdown. Tell him it would be easier to understand him if he took a couple breaths and just talked to you. If he makes specific threats, ask how he plans to carry out his threats. He may continue to threaten you, or he may calm down. Later, you'll write a classification input either way and keep him in Ad/Seg if he can't change his behavior.

More importantly, the rest of the inmates in the housing unit will be watching you and what they will see is a staff member who is not angry or affected in any way by the challenge. The inmates will do the same thing kids do at recess when it looks like there won't be a fight. They will lose interest and return to playing with their friends.

Inmates and admin expect and respect stability in correctional staff. Checking your ego in at the locker room will help you retain that stability and get you through your shift safer with less trouble from the inmates in your charge. If you have ever wondered why there are those staff members who have fewer issues with the inmate population, it very well could be that these correctional professionals have removed their ego from their jobs.

One of my partners (let's call him Joe) in the jail's housing units was a clean freak. Joe brushed his teeth at least twice during a 12-hour overnight shift. He washed his hands before *and* after he used the restroom. He double gloved on many occasions, and passionately encouraged others to do the same. Joe also focused on a clean jail.

Joe started every shift on the floor assigning cleaning projects. These projects were not a reaction to bad inmate behavior. He wasn't mean spirited when he delegated work to the inmates. When it came to these projects, Joe only raised his voice once a shift, to make the general announcement.

"OK, listen up!" Joe would pace the housing unit with his clipboard in one hand and a pen in the other. "Before you guys come off lockdown, this place needs to be clean." Joe would tell each inmate their specific cleaning assignments, and write each job on a list.

Once in a while, an inmate who hadn't been exposed to Joe would pipe up with a protest or remark. Generally, the inmate's cellmates would hush him for the sake of the group, but from time-to-time Joe would address the comment. I was present for one such address.

Joe strolled over to the inmate, stopping along the way to delegate cleaning projects. He didn't want the protester to think he was at the top of Joe's list.

"You don't want to clean?" Joe asked the question with a look of surprise on his face. "You don't like a clean cell?"

The inmate didn't have anything to say. As we all know, any prisoner worth his salt likes to keep a clean cell.

Joe continued, "I'm going to be here for the next 12 hours. This is my workplace. I need it to be clean for you and I need it to be clean for me, so I can do my job in a clean place and you can live in a clean place. Does that make sense to you?"

A couple hours later, and before the sergeant walked through for her inspection, Joe followed up with his list. Some inmates called him and ask if their cleaning project was good enough. The protester cleaned his cell. No one wants to be the odd man out.

Joe made no threats of discipline. He didn't push his authority around. The discipline and authority were implied the moment he walked in a housing unit. There's no need to lean on either until you've exhausted your well-honed verbal judo skills.

INMATES WON'T RESPECT WHAT YOU DON'T INSPECT

What Joe did was set a clear expectation of cleanliness early on in his shift. There was no question from the inmates as to Joe's intentions. Joe would further hold specific inmates responsible for their part in cleaning the housing unit. Finally, he would inspect for results and revisit any items on his list that were not addressed.

Joe didn't spend too much time on these projects. There was plenty more to do, but he followed up and moved on.

It's easy to waltz into a housing unit, announce the place looks dirty, and walk out. This drive-by method allows inmates to opt out without any personal skin in the game. Such a general announcement, with no specifics to back it up, leaves your communication up to interpretation.

An inmate will most likely take the path of least resistance, maybe saying, "Oh, the floor cop says this place is dirty. He must mean we need to wipe that one table over there in the corner. Done, I'm a hero!" Without specifics, the inmates will create their own expectations and they generally won't match yours.

The drive-by method of setting expectations is also easier for the floor officer. There is no follow-up necessary. You can tell yourself you've addressed an issue of cleanliness. You can even follow up with, "Yep, place looks better." But you haven't really addressed anything. You'll be leaving it to your supervisor to address the issues, or the next shift.

Inmates notice which staff members prefer the drive-by approach to running a housing unit. They take notice because staff members who phone it in on the simple stuff may also phone it in on contraband and jail rules.

Teachable moments

When Joe spoke to the protester, every ear within hearing range and some outside the range were perked, hoping to hear what Joe had to say. Joe was careful with his words. He knew any time he addressed an inmate in the presence of other inmates that he was essentially addressing everyone who could hear him.

This form of *very informal* public response to any public negative inmate behavior can be tricky, but very useful if you have complete control over your emotions. It's an opportunity to broadcast that you are unbending when an inmate protests your orders, but reasonable in your response to the protest.

If you feel this interaction will escalate to a challenge in any way, you're better off taking the conversation outside of the housing unit. Know the difference between a minor attempt to derail you from your mission and a direct challenge to your authority. A challenge should be addressed in a safe environment, fully controlled by staff.

Preemptive expectations

Expectations can extend to any behavior you can predict. For example, if you are escorting a group of inmates to court, you should expect some of their family members would be in court. You should also expect that, even when they know they shouldn't, the inmates may attempt to communicate with their family members.

Set behavior expectations in the few moments before entering court. Tell the inmates they are not allowed to talk to their families. They know that you know the rules, but when you specify your expectation, you're putting the inmates on notice that it is an important rule to you, and you'll be paying attention.

Because the reminder of the rule and expectation has been made so recently, you'll find it much simpler to address anyone who breaks the rules. You've already told them once. You've already created the unwritten contract to follow a specific rule.

The final hour

Inmates will try to get away with more at the end of your shift than they will at the beginning. You have very little time to follow up within the last hour of your shift, and there's less time to write reports. Time will be a huge challenge if you don't address expectations early on and give yourself time to revisit your expectations.

It's Friday morning and you have an hour left in your shift. The jail commander is about to walk through for his weekly inspection. This is not the time to gather up a cleaning crew to get your housing unit scrubbed, swept and mopped. You're too late. Plan ahead and set your expectations early.

Working nightshift in Main Jail years ago, I sat at the floor desk and heard a group of young inmates make so much noise that they were most likely keeping other inmates up. It wasn't a huge deal. No one was getting hurt, but I had to address the issue, as the noise would eventually cause an exchange of harsh words. Someone would say something they couldn't take back and I would end up having to investigate why Inmate Talksalot had a fresh black eye at the breakfast line the following morning.

I walked through the unit and formally told the loud group to quiet down. I didn't raise my voice. I didn't act hard with the inmates. I just gave them a quiet order to quiet down. They stopped long enough for me to finish my walk-through and picked back up as I sat at my desk. I returned to the group at my next walk-through and stepped it up a little, hoping they would understand me a little better. I tersely said, "Hey guys, this ain't romper room. There are other people trying to sleep. Pipe down!" There, I explained how their behavior was affecting others and used an increased level of command in my voice. This was sure to send a message and quiet the young group down.

The inmates lasted just a little longer this time, trying to keep their voices down, but increased their volume within 20 minutes. At this point I was irritated. I marched into the unit, faced the scofflaws, and said, "You guys need to SHUT THE F**K UP!" The inmates stopped talking and packed it in for the night. As I calmed my face and nodded my approval to their response, one of the inmates said, "Hey, Zaied, why didn't you say you wanted us to shut up in the first place?"

Control how you say it

There are plenty of moments in a correctional facility when communicating with inmates on their level will get you much further than talking to them as if you're talking to civilians at the grocery store or communicating with your family at home. There are times when you can make a conscious decision to change your speech patterns, your tone and your body language to mirror inmate behaviors so that they may understand you better.

More effective communication leads to better supervision in any situation, especially in a jail or a prison. What happens, however, when we lose our awareness of the changes in our communication styles?

How many times have you observed your fellow correctional staff changing their behavior patterns gradually over time after more and more exposure to inmates? Have you ever noticed yourself speaking differently at home after long weeks in the jail? On many occasions, I have stepped through my front door after work and started a conversation with a family member. Five minutes into the conversation, the family member would say, "Hey, relax, you're off duty. I'm not an inmate."

Internal social strength

There is a spectrum of strength related to our egos and standings within any group of people. Within a social setting, one key indicator of where we stand in the group is the unconscious mirroring of others. On the bottom of the spectrum is the individual who has no conviction of self and mimics the mannerisms, language and behaviors of others. On the top of the social spectrum is the unapologetic maverick who barely notices anyone else's behavior in the group and often comes up with sayings that become part of the group's vernacular.

About a year ago, I noticed a catchy phrase everyone started using at work in response to unbelievable stories we all heard at shift change. These are the stories unique to Corrections. The response was, "Checks out." The respondent was saying, "That may be unbelievable, but in our place of business, it's normal and it checks out."

The phrase spread quickly through the facility, first with staff, then to the inmate population. The phrase became part of the facility language. One staff member who happened to operate higher in the jail's social spectrum started the trend. I found myself using the phrase several times and had to explore the reason why.

What's important in a correctional setting is that when you speak with inmates, you sound like you and not like a product of your environment. When you walk through a housing unit, maybe you shouldn't thrust your hips forward and pivot your shoulders back and forth like a parolee walking down Main Street, unless that's how you really walk.

If you do decide to mirror inmate behavior and speech, make sure you do it to better communicate with the inmates. More important, change your behavior with the awareness that keeps you from falling into speech and body language patterns by matter of habit.

Communication as social response

There is a heightened level of awareness when we walk into a facility and even more so when we walk into a housing unit where staff are grossly outnumbered by inmates. Let that awareness serve to make sure you don't behave and speak in reaction to your environment. Worst, don't let the correctional environment shape you with just simple exposure. When you walk into a housing unit, it is your housing unit. The inmates in the unit are your guests. It is your house (more on this later). There should be some level of social comfort that you are in your own domain.

San Quentin is the oldest working prison in California. Sheriff's transport units from around the San Francisco Bay Area have brought groups of inmates to the regional reception center for decades. Vans line up and wait in a caged area to unload new commitments at the intake area.

The cage is surrounded by the hustle and bustle of daily prison life, with inmates coming and going to their housing units, exercising in the yard and socializing. The caged area gets a lot of attention from inmates, mostly because they want to know who is coming to prison and from which county.

I've seen more than once county jail Corrections staff waiting outside their vans behave in an overly boisterous manner, much like the inmates who get in the van at the county jail, preparing for their trip to prison. The inmates on that ride often talk excitedly about how much they know about prison and how wonderful it is to go to prison. In reality, a majority of the commitments are scared of what's to come. The inmates in the transport van always get quiet as the van approaches San Quentin's entry gate.

Who is in there?

I would argue the response to San Quentin is the same between the inmates who are arriving for the first time through the gothic prison gates and some county jail transport officers, who are out of their element. We compensate with confidence to impress on the inmates in the van or the inmates watching us in the yard that we are not scared of prison and all the social pressures prison comes with; that we don't have a care in the world as a hundred pair of eyes watch our every move. People behave differently as a response to social fear or discomfort.

Next time you are in a new correctional setting, surrounded by inmates you don't know, pay attention to your own behavior and make sure what and how you communicate with your words, body and face comes from who you are as opposed to your response to what your environment is.

I've noticed throughout the years that inmates generally walk in a counterclockwise circle when walking in the yard and in their dayrooms.

I commented on this phenomenon one day when I took a group of inmates to the yard. I started talking about habits and how hard they are to break. I challenged the group to walk the yard clockwise. They laughed and ignored the challenge, except one older inmate. He walked against the stream for two rounds. You would think the guy was juggling alligators. Other inmates looked at him as if he had joined the circus. The brave man quickly returned to his more comfortable counterclockwise walk. He commented that it was hard for him to be like a salmon.

Some of the inmates engaged in the conversation and wondered why they all walked counterclockwise. One took the conversation to the next level and asked the group if they thought inmates walk clockwise in Australia, comparing the pattern to draining water in a bathtub.

Learned habits in Corrections

Inmates get involved in many learned habits in a correctional setting. Some of these are as harmless as the direction they walk in the yard, while others can cause disruption, harm or extra costs to a correctional facility. A majority of bad inmate habits and behavior are the result of poor control measures by staff. While Corrections staff can use some inmate habits to the benefit of the facility, when bad habits become the new norm, it takes a coordinated approach to changing them.

Bad habits in action

Coming back to the jail from a multi-year transport detail, training officer Joe Smith, who happens to be a stickler for the rulebook, finds multiple inmates with rings on their fingers in the housing units. Joe is baffled as he knows this is against policy. What's more, he recently saw a memo by the lieutenant that all jewelry shall be removed at intake.

If Joe walks into a housing unit and starts removing rings, he's going to have a rough time, especially since staff members around him have ignored the issue for so long. Inmates will argue. In some way, since staff has allowed the habit, the inmates have a solid argument for keeping the rings. Intake staff let them keep the rings when the inmates arrived at the facility. Other staff have allowed inmates to keep the rings in the housing units. Even supervisors have walked through the housing units and didn't address the matter.

This is an issue that is created by staff. In Joe's case, any change would have to be made on a facility-wide basis with a plan set out by the facility administration and buy-in down the chain of command. Changing a widespread bad inmate habit takes a concerted effort. Taking advantage of existing habits, however, can be pretty easy and actually enjoyable.

How to take advantage of inmate habits

When you walk into a modular housing unit, where all of the cell doors face the entry door, a majority of the inmates who are mentally aware and awake will walk to their cell-door windows to see who is coming in. That said, if you have something important to tell the whole housing unit, maybe take advantage of the initial attention you already have when you first walk into the unit.

In my county jail's linear housing units, inmates line up for meals generally in the same order they did the previous day and generally they do so as their cell doors open. They also know what time they are scheduled to come off lockdown and when the television should be turned on. They know that when the television is turned off, most likely, they will need to lock down.

Inmates live by the clock and the more regularly you adhere to that clock, the harder they take it when you rearrange the time in which events will take place. For example, if you take a specific housing unit to yard right after medication pass every day for weeks, the inmates will line up for yard right after the nurse leaves the unit. They'll expect yard within a short time after medication pass. Conversely, if you feed your jail in a specific order every meal, inmates will expect to be fed in that order. If you regularly feed A-Pod first, then B-Pod, then C and finally D-Pod, C-Pod will never expect to be fed before B or after D.

Knowing when inmates all leave their cells gives Corrections staff great advantage when planning a search of a housing unit. Inmates are all lined up and outside their cells at a specific time. The shift supervisor can have extra staff at the ready and responding when the inmates are in their scheduled comfort zone. It's true, you can always order all the inmates out of their cells for mandatory yard, but they will flush contraband on their way out.

Keep in mind, if you surprise inmates in H-Module every Wednesday at lunch with a cell search, they'll quickly learn to bring their contraband with them to the chow line. It's in our nature as Corrections staff to schedule ourselves and sometimes, even our random surprises become predictable.

Inmates pay attention to shift changes, walk-throughs, inspections and any irregularities in the pattern.

There is a certain benefit, both to staff and inmates from repeating certain events in the same order every day. If we had to spell out every lockdown for a group of inmates because lockdown was at random times throughout the day, headcount would be a daily headache. This in fact rings true in mixed classification housing units where inmates have unscheduled lockdowns for movement or other reasons. Even if unscheduled lockdowns become a matter of regular practice, they still cause extra tension in a housing unit.

For correctional staff, not having to think creatively about what we will be doing next provides room in our creative bandwidth for more important matters. If the floor officer follows a repeated schedule, s/he can focus more on observing inmate behavior, or spend time in the housing unit, searching for contraband.

Inmates live a life filled with unknown court case dispositions, chaotic relationships and unpredictable living situations outside of custody. For the inmates, order and predictability provide some sense of safety. In knowing when he will be going to yard every day, an inmate will take comfort that yard is one thing that is not up in the air. Unfortunately, predictability also provides inmates with opportunity to engage in nefarious behavior.

When you need to be unpredictable

Scheduling certain events in specific predictable order throughout the day makes sense. Other predictable staff behaviors should include our reaction to bad behavior. What should not be predictable is how often you walk through a unit and how long you walk through a unit. Facility perimeter checks should be conducted at different times, not just first thing after shift change, after lunch and sometime before dinner. If you have a partner and you take turns walking the unit, try walking the unit together and coming out at different times, or having one follow the other five minutes after.

When you walk into a housing unit, try not to walk the same way. You can walk directly to the back of a linear unit and zigzag back from cell to cell. You can start with the higher number cells instead of walking from one to two to three and so forth. Instead of conducting cell inspections first thing on shift, try inspecting cells several at a time, as you conduct longer, more meaningful walkthroughs.

One side benefit to changing up your duty habit where you can is that your brain will remain more engaged in your duties. Pay very close attention if you just did a walk through and, like driving home, the action becomes as much a routine as breathing. This would be a good time to stay on your toes and change what you can to remain engaged. Inmates will take advantage of a passively engaged housing deputy.

Finally, there's nothing wrong with changing up the order of events in your jail from time to time. Sure, it may cause disruption, but if you're ready with good reasons and the ability to address possible inmate agitation, a little periodic schedule scramble can help inmates think twice about counting on a schedule for nefarious purposes.

Surprise the housing unit that gets fed last every day with the first hot lunch trays. They will be thrilled and tell you what a great human being you are. This will later be followed by, "I thought you were cool!" when you search their cells. The inmates in the traditional first unit to be fed may balk. You really don't owe them any explanation, but these matters can be easily addressed with humor or an emphatic call for fairness.

Habits can help Corrections staff and they can hurt us. Regardless of how you handle inmate habits, it's important to be aware of them. More important, it is crucial for Corrections staff members to be aware of our own habits, good and bad.

"Are you working the floor today? Bring a can of 'Leg-Off' with you."

We've all heard the warnings at shift change, or while running special assignments. Inmates are a needy group. They need toilet paper, they need their meds, a Band-Aid, yard time. For a deputy on the floor, the requests are singular and simple to address. However, the more decision-making power you have as an individual, the more you're going to hear your name called out.

While assigned to classification, I walked into an administrative segregation unit one morning. I had a list of inmates to speak with and a tight schedule. I was already behind for the week. This was going to be the day I caught up. Sound familiar?

One wide-eyed inmate with hopes he would get good news that day called my name. He called it very loudly and made enough of an echo to wake the unit. I ignored him. Two others called my name and I waved them off, focused on the path I had set to complete my mission. With increasing sincerity and intensity, more inmates called my name to the point I was becoming distracted.

I looked around and found a few inmates laughing while they called my name. They didn't need anything. They just saw me start to get distracted and wanted to watch the show. They got me!

I took a breath, got my composure back, and sang out, "Say my name, say my name" in a pretty good falsetto. I got a collective laugh and even a few claps. More important, I got control of the unit back with a bit of humor.

I addressed what was happening, I responded to it in a creative manner, and I continued on with my day, avoiding a potentially large and unnecessary detour.

The value of time spent listening

Talking to inmates is a much simpler proposition in direct supervision facilities. Staying focused on one unit allows you the time to remain engaged with the inmates. That same confined space can test your patience meter. Inmates have the opportunity to chip at you all day and, in some cases, for an entire six-month rotation in a housing unit.

In a setting where you're walking through housing units for minutes on the hour, it's much easier to wave off inmate attempts to engage you. You can blow inmates off with, "Not now, I've got a lot to do, gotta go, here's a request form." You can move on and stay off radar for a majority of the shift.

But you're building overall discontent and pressure you may be passing on to a team member at shift change or back onto yourself the following day.

The three minutes you invest by stopping and talking to any inmate is the hour you may save later in the day by not having to address bad behavior or a fight and most definitely a report. You can answer most questions within those three minutes and often respond to simple requests with yes or no

Even if what the inmate wants is outside what you're willing or able to give, your time spent listening will pay dividends. You're showing the inmate you care enough to stop and listen. You've already done your duty. At this point, you can say no, as long as you are not in "Auto-No" mode.

How (and why you want to) explain "no"

You don't have to explain your "no" answers, but what if you do?

Try following up with, "You've been doing time longer than me, Smith, you know better." Or, "I'm not giving you an extra pair of socks because I don't have an extra pair for Jones or Ford over there."

In this case, you demonstrate your refusals come from a reasonable place and you're not just saying no automatically. More important, you are giving a little extra time to the inmate.

You can apply the same method to any inmate attempts to manipulate you with a positive interaction. You just said yes to Inmate Taylor's request and Taylor follows up with, "See, I told you guys Officer Bell is the good one. *He's the only one who really cares about us.*"

Taylor is hoping you will do something for him no one else will do, most likely something against your facility policy. In ignoring Taylor, you don't give yourself the opportunity to call him out on his manipulation efforts. You may also be demonstrating you are not smart enough to see what he's doing. The inmates may think you're too lazy to address the comment. Worst, now Inmate Taylor thinks you may be uncomfortable with confrontation.

Respond with something witty, serious, or any other appropriate comment from your tool bag. Even if you've used the same response a hundred times, you're demonstrating you know what Inmate Taylor is up to, showing you're not afraid of what he's up to, and communicating to Taylor and his palls that the con is not effective. Most important, you have responded and remained engaged.

A danger to your facility

Disengaged Corrections staff become a target for inmate tests. If you ignore the little things, inmates will want to know what else you will ignore. Your shifts will become harder as you move through, ignoring increasingly intensified attempts by inmates to push your limits and bend or break rules.

A disengaged staff member spells good news for any inmate with plans to avoid detection. Whether the inmate is hiding alcohol in a cell, or making plans to bring in a weapon from the yard, he will count on a disengaged staff member to allow success in his nefarious plans.

A disengaged staff member makes life more difficult for proactive staff members by creating an example to the inmates that is bad for staff, but good for any inmates who want to break rules.

The inmates learn to expect a lower level of care and become incredulous when a proactive staff member conducts a random cell search for contraband. Most of this inmate reaction is fabricated to make you uncomfortable, but some of it comes from the comparison they get to make between the proactive staff member and the "cool guard" who doesn't care.

We've all had those moments where we were too busy to stop, or just needed a break from endless inmate requests. It's ok to check out for a few moments, take a walk, or spend a break talking to your partner about anything but work. Disengage away from inmates, but when you return, stay on point

The payoff

Think back to a moment in your facility when a group of inmates were out of control. Maybe they were protesting cold showers, they felt slighted, or the air conditioning didn't work. Before the SERT team marched in, jail staff made attempts to communicate with the group and address the incident peacefully. Who did the inmates demand to speak with?

In some cases, inmates ask for a sergeant or lieutenant. Often, they'll ask for specific line staff members. Sure, sometimes it's just a game to see how many hoops staff will run through, but when the inmates are actually angry, they want to talk with someone who has a history of successful communications during difficult incidents in the jail.

If you establish a history of engaged interactions with inmates, you will be rewarded with the benefit of two-way communication. When there is a legitimate problem brewing in a housing unit, inmates seek out engaged staff members. The staff member who cares enough to stop and talk to inmates about their next court date is the same staff member who will pause to address issues before they blow up or before control of an inmate group is about to fall apart.

You walk into a housing unit to conduct a walk-through. Inmate Jones meets you at the front door to the unit with a very important question, as evidenced by the concern on his face. Jones wants to know when he will be going to court. He presents a complex arrest timeline, and he thinks he may have been over detained. This is a matter of emergency and, also, his son's birthday is today, and he really needs you to look into this right now!

Inmate Jones has been doing time longer than you have been employed in the jail. He has the court's arraignment calendar committed to memory and doesn't actually have a son. The level of urgency in his voice and his mannerisms are manufactured. If you tell him you can look into his concern in 10 minutes, he may balk a little, but he will return to his cell and he will have done his job.

In Jones' case, there was actually an emergency of sorts. Three of his buddies had lost track of time and you were early for your walk-through because you don't like to be predictable. The three had a bag of Pruno cooking in a sink full of warm water and the bag had expanded from the fermentation process. The cooks really needed to "burp" the bag, but you would have smelled the fumes as you walked by their cell.

Why inmates stop you at the door

Inmates often find reasons to approach you or call you to a cell for a conversation when you walk into your housing unit. Inmates sometimes engage in meaningless conversations, or ask you complex questions, slowing you down at the front door.

When you first walk into your unit for the shift, an inmate may engage you just to check your temperature. They may truly want to know if you are in a good mood or bad mood (there shouldn't be a difference). Inmates want to know how the next 12 hours are going to go for them and housing officers have a big effect on how the day will go.

An inmate may be starved for attention and looking for some connection to society. Housing staff is often that inmate's strongest connection to the community. That inmate who wants to talk about the weather or the latest championship game may just be checking in for some validation that they are still part of something.

These small exchanges are opportunities for staff to shore up an individual's sense of relevance and build good will with a member of the inmate population. However, it is important to remember that your kindness can also be seen as an opening for inmates to attempt manipulation. Always pay closer than normal attention to a request from an inmate that comes after you have had a positive exchange with that inmate.

An inmate may try to get your attention because they are in danger or has a friend who is in danger in the housing unit. Inmates generally have a strong aversion to asking staff for help. It is often the socially higher functioning inmates who approach you and engage you in conversation. When an inmate meaninglessly engages you, who doesn't fit in with any groups, or seems to be socially uncomfortable in your housing unit, pay close attention as this inmate could be in trouble with the other inmates. You may want to find a reason to remove the inmate from the housing unit and have a private conversation.

Ruin the interference – Keep walking

Finally, you may be getting stopped at the door by *the good neighbor*, an inmate who rings the alarm and buys time for other inmates to cover up nefarious activities in the housing unit. This inmate will be very friendly and boisterous, sounding the sophisticated version of "hot water!" just in case his neighbors need a little extra time to hide whatever it is they shouldn't be doing. He may have a manufactured urgent matter to stop you from walking. He may not have anything made up and just call you over, just to buy a little more time for other inmates to cover up blood from a fight or evidence of contraband.

Each time I come across the good neighbor, I think of my long-time sergeant's story of his old army colonel. The colonel was always on the move and if you ever tried to stop him with an issue or a question, he would ask, "Can you walk and talk?" The soldiers in the regiment called him "Colonel Walk-and-Talk."

When an inmate addresses me during a walk-through of my housing unit, I ask, "Can you walk and talk?" Then I keep moving. This gives me a chance to remain engaged with the inmate. He may actually have something important to talk about. Even if what he is doing is running interference, I don't want to ignore the inmate completely. He may choose to walk with me, at which point, I may jokingly ask him if he is escorting me through the housing unit. Now he knows that I know he may be the good neighbor. Once I'm done walking through the housing unit, I can stop and take my time addressing in earnest any questions the inmates may have.

This isn't an emergency

Regardless of why an inmate who is not in danger attempts to stop you with conversation during your walk-through, you can keep moving. You can give the inmate a choice to wait a few minutes for your full attention or walk with you as he addresses you. You maintain control of your duty timeline.

When you keep moving past potential distractions, you broadcast your intentions to maintain the safety and security of your housing unit. Your priority to be watchful of the housing unit will give inmates second thoughts when they attempt to engage in nefarious activity and, when you walk past the good neighbor, inmates will lose faith in their alarm system.

"Get out of my house!"

The inmate yelled out in the deepest voice he could come up with. I was searching his cell and he was sitting in the day room, playing cards, 20 feet away. I paused for a second before I continued, then quietly laughed at myself for considering if I was invading someone's private space. This was exactly what the inmate wanted, to make me uncomfortable doing my job. I had to remind myself that this was my house.

Don't be a guest

Inmates are tuned in to the level of ownership you feel for the correctional facility you are tasked with running. If they see you feel like a guest in a housing unit, they will take advantage of your discomfort and cultivate a separation between you and your duties.

Inmates also pay close attention to the level of ownership you take when you enforce facility rules. If you hesitate while correcting behavior in a housing unit, inmates will test your level of commitment by not responding the first time you give them orders.

When you walk into a housing unit and inmates are standing around in the day room, do you address them first, or do they address you first? When you walk into that housing unit, do you feel you are walking into their living space, or is this your housing unit? If you enter a cell and an inmate half jokingly demands a warrant, what's your response? How quickly do you make it clear that the inmate is a guest in a jail cell owned by the taxpayers?

Own your interactions

If you don't feel like you're walking into your own domain when entering a housing unit, you'll have to fake it until you deal with any anxieties connected with entering socially hostile spaces.

Pretend you're walking into the place you feel most socially comfortable, but don't confuse comfort with relaxation. As you know, you should never be so comfortable in a correctional setting that you become relaxed and complacent.

There is a social advantage to addressing others before they address you when you walk into a new space. As the initiator of any social interaction, you get to set the tone of the conversation. By asking the first question, you place the respondent in a socially defensive position, as they must fill the social cue to answer the question. As you walk into a housing unit, a simple "How are you?" or "Who's winning the game?" can set that tone.

Pay attention to where you fit in during a social interaction the next time someone initiates a conversation with you. If they ask you a question and you are responding, are you in a position of social offense or social defense? If you answer the question and follow up with a question for the initiator, are the two of you now more even on the social scale?

Social hierarchy is often defined on a microcosmic level by who is asking the questions and who is answering them. This can be seen more plainly in news interviews and criminal investigations, or when a teen comes home and dad asks, "How was school today?" In initiating a conversation, you become the owner of that conversation. When you do so in a correctional setting, you shore up your ownership of any housing unit you walk into, adding to your level of authority.

Own your job duties

Ownership in a correctional setting goes beyond conversations between staff members and inmates. When chain of command and unity play an integral part of effecting staff control of a facility, it is important that Corrections staff members take ownership when enforcing facility rules.

Command staff periodically see enforcement of a rule fall short or stop completely. They will task shift supervisors with renewed efforts to get the facility back on track. When directives are handed down the chain of command to reinforce rules, inmates count on the housing officers to hesitate in their enforcement efforts.

There is a marked difference between telling the inmates in a housing unit that the sergeant wants all cell property put away in lockers and telling the inmates that **you** want all cell property put away in lockers. Inmates know very well where changes in enforcement come from, but that doesn't stop them from testing your commitment to that enforcement.

When you take full ownership of your duties, regardless of where the order originated, you will curb that inmate testing.

As a classification officer, I was ordered by the classification sergeant to move an inmate from one housing unit to another. He had received information from a shift supervisor that prompted the move. I stood at the inmate's door and told him to roll up his belongings and be ready to move. The inmate asked me who made the decision. I told him my supervisor made the decision and he didn't have a choice. The inmate demanded to speak with the classification sergeant before he moved.

This scenario could have gone much differently had I taken ownership of the command. Inmates don't need to know at what level decisions are made. I learned to lead with full ownership of an order in future incidents. The answer to whose decision it is to execute an order falls directly on the staff member giving the order to an inmate. You tell the inmate, "I'm moving you to another housing unit." When they ask who made the decision, you can simply say, "This is my decision." You're not lying. You have decided to follow orders to move this inmate to another housing unit.

You can always point inmates to your facility's appeal process. In the end, the inmate may have an opportunity to plead his case with your supervisor, but not because he demands to talk to the sergeant in order to follow your direct orders.

Another tactic inmates use when challenging your commitment to enforcement is fishing for your opinion on the rule you are enforcing. You can prevent this by stating you are not employed to like or dislike rules. Inmates will ask your opinions in many situations.

If you want to engage in an opinion conversation for the sake of comedic relief of institutional tension, you can always change a fact into an opinion. For example, "It is my opinion you will get a write up if you don't lock down for count," or, "It is my strong opinion that it may rain tomorrow."

This is Your House

Staff ownership of a correctional facility and its rules will lead to fewer challenges from the inmate population and less time spent negotiating with difficult inmates. It will also reduce the opportunity for inmates to find weak links in the chain of command. Maintaining that ownership as a matter of operational baseline creates an environment where staff works more effectively while dealing with difficult inmates and new institutional rules.

Think back to your first day when you got off training. Untethered to the security of a training officer, you walk into briefing, receive a set of keys and a radio, then off you go to face 50 or more inmates. You're armed with several weeks of knowledge to navigate your day. You have the daily housing schedule down, you know how to inspect a cell and you've memorized the visiting schedule.

You walk into your assigned housing unit and start an initial headcount. You hear one inmate ask his cellmate, "Who's *this* guy?" He says it loud enough for you to hear. You walk onward past another cell and the testing continues. An inmate asks you when the unit will come out for program. Another inmate asks you why he has not been taken to court yet. A third inmate tells you he should have been released, time served, hours ago!

Two friendly inmates in Cell-216 engage you in conversation. One asks how long you've been working at the jail. The other asks what your first name is.

The first inmate gives you his approval, "You seem pretty cool. You have a nice day, CO." He sends you off.

You finish your headcount and walk to your desk. An inmate you passed by just moments ago stands at his cell door and yells at you, "CO! CO! I need a towel and a pair of boxers!" The man acts like he's having an emergency and becomes irritated when you sit at your desk and acknowledge his request with a head nod and thumbs up instead of filling his request right away.

They're taking your temperature

Inmates often check on Corrections staff early on during a shift. They want to know what they can get away with, and if rules will be enforced. Inmates want to know if staff will be responsive to their needs or if the floor officer will blow off requests. Sometimes, they just want to see if they can distract you with small tasks, or somehow affect your day.

The longer you work at any facility and the more consistent you are with your responses and reactions to questions, the less chance the inmates will test you unnecessarily. But for the new Corrections deputy or officer, inmates want to know what reaction they will get to their questions and challenges.

The inmate who says something derogatory to another inmate within your earshot is actually speaking directly to you. He wants to see how you will react if he says something about you or asks a question meant for you. He feels pretty safe testing the waters this way, because he can always say he wasn't talking to you. If the inmate wants to test you further in this way, he will say something inappropriate about one of your fellow staff members.

Most of the inmates who ask you about schedules and court dates have been "doing time" longer than you. They know when the housing unit comes off lockdown. They know the court schedule. The unreleased inmate is not asking why he hasn't been released. He is asking if booking found the warrant in the system from two counties away. Inmates are testing what you know and how you respond if you don't know.

An inmate with a non-emergency emergency may actually feel like it's an emergency that he doesn't have a towel. Maybe he has asked the last three staff members who walked through for a towel without response. More likely, that inmate wants to push your response timeline and pressure you to respond faster than you need to a simple request.

The two nice inmates who give you positive feedback on job performance may be cultivating you with social judgment – *You seem pretty cool.* Maybe they actually mean well and want to promote goodwill with you. It's possible. It's also possible the two are trying to create an environment in which they can get unreasonable favors from you. Any time an inmate initiates a positive interaction with you, keep in mind he may follow up with a favor request. If the request is reasonable and you say yes, there may be an unreasonable request coming.

The inmate who asks your first name doesn't care about your first name. My favorite response when an inmate asks me what the Z in Z. Zaied stands for. My reply, "It stands for deputy." The response generally gets a chuckle from an inmate, but sends a clear message. Let's face it, anyone can find out your first name. We use them when we testify. Our first names sometimes appear on official paperwork and on the internet.

Our first names are not highly guarded secrets. In a Corrections setting, however, the social interaction associated with asking and finding out the first name crosses barriers and turns a formal environment into an informal one. This is why we address inmates by their last names. Consequently, I've found using first names is useful when addressing inmates who are experiencing mental distress due to mental health issues or drug use.

The inmate who dismisses you from his presence before you disengage is attempting a small power play. Find a subtle reason to extend your presence and control when you leave.

Check your ego at the gate

After 16 years in Corrections, I still don't have all the answers. I don't need to have all the answers. After California rolled out the Prison Realignment Act, many prison inmates ended up in local jails. During the transition, many inmates made requests for paperwork identified differently by the prison system. Jail staff did not know what they were asking for. A common incredulous response from an inmate would be, "You don't know what that is!?"

The funniest response I heard to the small attempt at a power play was, "No, this is a jail, you're here because the State of California has determined you're not hard enough for state prison." I don't recommend this specific response because at its core, the comment encourages state prison bound behavior. The point, however, is that Corrections staff shouldn't be embarrassed not knowing something. Don't let an inmate try to shame you for not knowing something, especially if you don't need to know it.

Don't hesitate to tell and inmate you don't know something. Be confident telling an inmate that you don't know the answer, but make sure you follow up with, "I can find out," or "I'll get back to you." Then do what you've promised, but do it on your own timeline, not one created by the inmate. An inmate's need for instant gratification is no reason to prioritize his need.

This is how it's done

Inmates love to train new guards or offer up information on "how things are done around here." Some inmates give you good information, and some give you bad information. Don't discount anything an inmate tells you about how things are done, but always double check what they tell you. This serves two purposes.

You want to encourage the inmate who gives you good information to continue. Maybe, down the road, the inmate will tell you something more critical to facility safety or smooth running. Indicating to inmates that you don't trust anything they say will close off any useful lines of communication.

You want to know which inmates will give you bad information so you can flag them for potential negative behavior down the road. It will be obvious if you believe them or not as you will have not followed bad advice. Ignoring bad information puts an inmate on notice that you are paying attention and may serve to deter future nefarious activity.

Some facilities have used inmates in the past to help train staff. While this may be a very real way to create training scenarios, there can be several negative outcomes. First, the inmates get insight on the facility's systems and first-hand knowledge of staff situational responses. Second, the inmates used to train staff feel they have an undue stake in the running of the facility. Finally, using inmates to teach lessons to staff has the potential to create unnecessary animosity between the two groups.

The more you know

For so many reasons, you should remain curious and actively seek out as much information about your facility as possible. Do this as soon as you walk in the door and don't quit being curious until the day you retire.

In the case of inmates testing you, they will stop testing you much quicker when they see you have a good knowledge base. Once they test you less, you'll find inmates will ask you more legitimate questions and respect you for having the answers. Having good command of your policies and procedures further allows you to quickly respond in a definitive manner to an inmate who challenges your decisions.

As you know more information about your correctional facility and have ready, meaningful responses to address questions and challenges, you'll find your job confidence will get a boost. Better mental confidence translates to how you carry yourself in the facility. Inmates will read your confident body language and test you less.

What time is it?

Inmates ask us questions for many different reasons. They often have legitimate questions. Be aware in many cases, an inmate has ulterior motives for asking a question. Any Inmate-initiated interaction has potential to be a test or setup

One inmate question I haven't figured out yet is, "What time is it?" I know inmates don't have watches and they most likely legitimately want to know what time it is. Most events in a Corrections facility run on a clock.

I can't help think, however, that there are other reasons inmates ask what time it is. Perhaps for some of the same reasons they ask any questions, to find out staff's level of willingness to be helpful.

When political discourse follows you to work

You see it in the news. Social media channels are saturated with it. Your local city and county governments are already contemplating new measures to address what appears to be on everybody's mind. You even hear family members and acquaintances talk about what can be done to fix law enforcement in the United States.

You are a resilient person. You were hired because you have the will to keep performing your job correctly when times are tough, but between your snooze alarm and the moment you hit the entry gate into your correctional institution, you've been exposed to multiple opinions on how you should do your job better. You are being told that law enforcement is racist and heavy-handed, and that agencies operate in the shadows, with little transparency and no oversight. This conversation has been a part of the American culture for decades.

After briefing, you head into your assigned housing unit for a headcount. Halfway through your count, you hear one inmate tell another, loud enough for you to hear him clearly, "I'm telling you, jail cops are just as bad as their brothers and sisters on the street." The inmate makes eye contact with you as you pass by and he finishes his statement. "These racists just **look** for reasons to knock you down."

What do you do?

Inmates will add fuel to the fire

You have had enough of this anti-law enforcement rhetoric. Your correctional institution is your domain. You don't need to hear this stuff at work too! Do you escort the inmate out of the housing unit and explain to him that you will not allow him to disparage Corrections staff? Do you give him a verbal warning or a write up? Do you respond with facts and set him straight? Do you quote your policies and offer up some supporting statistics?

These may be questions you are asking yourself as you hear an inmate disparage law enforcement, but there are a couple of other questions you should be asking yourself instead.

When the politics of the community enter your institution and inmates echo anti-law enforcement sentiment in your presence, ask yourself *why* an inmate is vocalizing the sentiment. In some cases, an inmate may be speaking from a personal experience and projecting that experience on anybody he sees wearing a badge. In many other cases, an inmate will see an opportunity to get an easy reaction from Corrections staff.

An inmate is banking on your emotions

Inmates in your facility will echo anti-law enforcement sentiment for the same reason they disparage Corrections staff when there is no public outcry about police in the news. An inmate may be trying to get a rise out of you, getting the satisfaction of an emotional response from a Corrections officer. In the current climate, an inmate knows it will be much easier to irritate you when you have been hearing the same negative sentiment in the news, on social media and from people around you. The goal is an emotional response from staff. It doesn't matter what the subject matter is.

Another inmate comment will be a seemingly positive one. The inmate will disparage law enforcement, except you and your partners, "because you're different," "you treat us right," or "you are not like them." Maybe the inmate is pointing to a partial truth and it is a matter of pride in your institution that you are able to maintain order without much force, or that you mix in some kindness and empathy while still maintaining control of the inmate population.

Pay close attention to the moment an inmate points out your accomplishments and compares you with other groups in the justice system. Be very aware that this can be the beginning of an attempted manipulation. The inmate is stroking your ego and, at the same time, trying to inspire a philosophical separation between you and other members of the justice system.

It's *why* they talk to you

Remember that the subject matter is much less important than the reasons behind why an inmate communicates with you. Whether an inmate is trying to get an immediate emotional reaction out of you, or set you up for the long con, your response should be the same. Just like you would on any normal day, keep your emotions out of the exchange.

If you get angry, proud, or defensive when you have an exchange with an inmate, you've already lost that exchange. You should <u>maintain an outwardly emotional distance</u> when responding to any inmate behavior. In times when law enforcement is under the microscope and you feel some extra stress from outside your facility, be mindful about your response to inmates inside your facility.

Take control of the conversation

You may not want to ignore an inmate who is trying to make a disparaging statement to you, directly or indirectly; especially if he is trying to insult you. You don't even have to stop a walk-through for a simple observation. Say, "That man has an opinion." The reply is not an insult and it's not emotional. It sounds like a compliment, but it's a subtle way of saying that the inmate is making a statement of opinion, NOT a statement of fact. Most importantly, you're not engaging in political discourse with the inmate.

An inmate may ask you for your opinion about a social movement to make radical changes to law enforcement or any other political hot topic of the day. The rules about personal opinions apply across the board in Corrections. You don't get paid to have an opinion. You are not going to share your serious opinions with inmates, unless there's an institutional benefit to doing so. You can simply advise the inmate that your opinion is not part of the job description.

If an inmate pushes for your opinion and you feel like engaging in some way, tell him, "You know, I do have an opinion, I think it might rain next week." In a nutshell, you have told the inmate that opinions on matters of fact are not very useful. Further, that even some facts are subject to change, as meteorologists know all too well. You may get a puzzled look from the inmate or a chuckle from his cellmate. You are also making it clear that you are not going to be pulled into a discussion of political opinions.

This is not the first time inmates have weighed in on the social discourse that affects the Corrections profession. Maintain a consistent response to inmate behavior, regardless of any connection to events outside your facility. Remember that inmates will try to find the easiest way to get an emotional response from you. If you are experiencing stress as a result of the current national conversation, pay closer attention with your responses to inmate manipulations and hold the line.

An inmate approaches you in your minimum-security housing unit. He chats you up a bit, telling you about his challenges. He tells you about what's going on with his family on the outside, his dreams and his hopes, and how he still has a year until his out date. You listen to the inmate and offer some empathy for his situation. You encourage him to keep working on himself and get back on his feet.

At this point, you are using your communication skills to build rapport. This is a positive contact. You're doing your part for the rehabilitation component of Corrections.

The inmate then tells you you're a good person and opines that you must truly care about the human beings under your care. Now, your observation skills kick in and your response to this inmate changes.

You maintain your professional demeanor, but bells ring in the back of your head. It could be that the inmate really means what he just said. If this guy is just having a positive reaction to your level of caring, then good for you for building some positive capital within the inmate population.

Then, while he figures that you are now emotionally connected with him, the inmate drops the question. "Hey, man." (Informal, because you're friends now, right?). "The game is on past lockdown today. Any chance we could keep the TV on during count? I tried asking the control officer, but he said you're running the show." (The ego boost because you're the boss.)

There it is. He was just working you for a small favor. Maybe that would have worked on a rookie, but not you. You have been trained on this stuff. You have read articles about *downing the duck*. You know the *games inmates play*. You're irritated and tell him to get lost. You say to yourself, "Next time, just cut that friendly talk out when it starts, and move on.

These inmates have all day to figure out ways to take down your defenses." You determine you will build up your defensive shell for the next time an inmate tries to play you with a positive conversation.

However, before you come across this kind of inmate again, ask yourself if you are able to be both hard-shelled AND show care at the same time. Can you fend off an inmate's manipulation attempt, while maintaining a positive exchange with that same inmate?

The correctional response spectrum

We have a spectrum of responses to different inmate behaviors. It takes good training and experience for most of us to fill that spectrum with the tools we need every day to respond appropriately as inmate behavior changes from hour to hour, from inmate to inmate, and from unit to unit.

With time, we learn to adjust our response level on that spectrum, increasing and lowering the level of intensity as circumstances develop. On one side of this sliding scale is the positive response to a well-behaved inmate who is just having a short conversation with you in passing. On the other side, is a call for backup and you going hands-on with a combative inmate. In between are all the different response mindsets we have to put ourselves into to function properly in a prison or a jail and to manage an inmate population that greatly outnumbers Corrections staff.

When we de-escalate a scared mental health patient, we use a different tone of voice and different words than the average inmate. The angry gang member, who didn't get his visits this week, requires a completely different attitude, choice of words and level of command presence than the inmate worker who didn't make his bunk.

Combining your responses

Beyond this spectrum are high-functioning Corrections officers who can pick and choose multiple tools from the spectrum of response and apply them at the same time. The farther on the spectrum from each other these deployed tools are, the more focused you have to be to effectively use them in combination.

Next time you find yourself in a seemingly harmless exchange with a relaxed inmate, don't be afraid to show some empathy and kindness. At the same time, keep your guard up and make sure the inmate knows you have not let your guard down. The old adage, "Don't confuse my kindness for weakness" is exactly what your expressions and body language should project.

Most important, stay away from the sarcasm that inmate games can build in Corrections staff. Sarcasm is an easy way to respond to a difficult reality, but if an inmate sees you have built a level of sarcasm into your demeanor, he will know the job and the inmate population has affected you and that you lack internal fortitude.

Instead of sarcasm, maintain vigilance, while exchanging a few kind words with an inmate. You will serve two important functions. You will project internal fortitude – a defense against inmate mind games – and you will, at the same time, build a positive moment with the inmate. When repeated, this process spreads a safer environment in your facility. At the same time, the mix of kindness and vigilance gives inmates fewer opportunities to find ways to get staff in trouble.

The professional

A local police officer once brought an arrestee into our local county jail. The arrestee became combative with Corrections staff right away and the arresting officer stayed on to assist. As the team worked to control the fighting arrestee, the arresting officer engaged, along with the team. Without losing any amount of intensity in his work to control the arrestee, the arresting officer talked to the arrestee in a reassuring tone and told him no one wanted to hurt him.

The arresting officer's language, tone of voice and expressions were pulled from the opposite end of the response spectrum than his physical response to the arrestee. He was completely in control of his tools and the arresting officer was effective, not letting the incident affect his abilities. What's more, the video and audio recording of the incident left no question that the officer was in control of his emotions and had no intention of harming the combative arrestee.

A true professional has the ability to employ many response tools at the same time when interacting with inmates. The ability to dynamically use multiple tools from your response spectrum takes focus and intent. In doing so, your response to any situation, whether it is a simple conversation, or a use of force incident, will be more effective and ultimately keep you safer and out of trouble.

A bad outcome from good intentions

Central Control has just announced there's a fight in the Special Housing Unit yard. Per policy, the floor officer is already waiting at the yard door for backup and the sergeant before he enters the yard.

You arrive at the housing unit's entry door as you hear the floor officer yell out, "He's going to kill that guy!"

The floor officer convinces Central Control to open the door and rushes into the yard as you and your partners cover the 80 feet to back him up.

At the yard door, you see two inmates have turned on the floor officer as you arrive. The inmates knock the floor officer down to the ground and start kicking him. Your group rushes to the yard. After a minute's struggle, you manage to control the two inmates. The sergeant arrives with more backup, but the incident has been resolved.

One of your partners is limping. He is sent for a checkup and comes back with his knee wrapped in ice. The floor officer is a bit shaken, but unharmed.

He feels guilty that one of his partners got injured, blaming himself. Within a week, other staff members play armchair quarterback and blame him too. The disciplinary lieutenant officially determines the floor officer and the control officer are to blame and should have managed the incident differently.

In the aftermath, the floor officer receives a written reprimand for rushing into an inmate fight without backup. The Central Control officer receives a written reprimand for opening the yard door prematurely. The 24-year-old officer who was injured, with three years into his career, has shattered his left knee badly enough that he may not return to work.

Discussions around the break room focus on other areas to place blame. People blame the training sergeant for not keeping staff trained with less than lethal weapons. Others identify staff shortages and blame low pay.

Your facility's morale takes a hit as some line staff members are bitter at the written reprimands. Other staff members blame lack of training for the outcome of the incident, and others express a lack of trust for the level of backup they receive from their partners when responding to incidents.

The facility's administration reacts with new directives to avoid the same outcome in the future. Line staff see the directives as a punishment for an incident most staff would have responded to in the same way. Morale dips some more and you can hear a lack commitment to the job and a lack of trust in radio traffic. Divisions start to form within the facility; between shifts, within shifts, and between line staff and command staff. You wonder how this all could have been avoided.

Negative reactions to bad outcomes

Incidents in correctional facilities that cause staff injury and death, create reactionary policy, or otherwise end in negative outcomes for seemingly sound decisions can have a long-lasting negative impact on a jail if the proper steps are not taken shortly after these critical incidents occur.

Your facility may have a full debriefing process after critical incidents, or maybe the sergeant just checks in with the parties involved and makes sure no one got hurt. Regardless, you will have to actively participate in any effort your institution makes to bounce back from a critical incident. Beyond helping your institution recover from a bad outcome, you will support your own quick recovery from the incident.

Corrections deputes make split-second decisions on a regular basis, often without the benefit of time to formulate a plan. In the case of the floor officer above, he decided to safeguard the life of an inmate. Command staff didn't agree with the floor officer's assessment, resulting in a reprimand.

Moving forward from a bad outcome in your facility is one of the most important skills you can develop to maintain a high level of resiliency. You may feel you made a bad call, or lay awake at home, reliving the "what ifs" of any situation. Otherwise, you may feel your actions were justified, but your supervisor feels you made a bad call and now you're in trouble.

Find the silver lining in any bad incident

It is very easy to blame yourself when the outcome of your actions produces a critical incident, even if there was no way to predict the outcome. It's easy to blame your partners, lack of training, lack of equipment, bad policy and command staff. Ask yourself, however, what all the blame is accomplishing. When you have finished a griping session in the breakroom, what tangible solution have you produced? Pointing a finger in any direction will leave you in the exact same spot you were when you started pointing.

When you are disappointed with the outcome of an incident, remember that there was a complex set of events and factors that ended in that outcome. Remove yourself from the incident and pick it apart, from start to finish. Remove any emotional response you have about the outcome for the sake of dissecting the incident and for the purpose of figuring out what went wrong.

Next, recreate the incident in your mind. Start with what went well and what you would have done again the same way. Then ask yourself if there was anything you, or anyone could have done differently to change the outcome. Make a list of the steps you would take before any similar incident in the future to change the outcome. Write yourself a narrative of the incident and your final thoughts, and include the good, bad and ugly.

You may find there were some actions you took that could have just produced different outcomes due to the elements of an incident that were out of your control.

Without placing blame, discuss the incident with your partners in an informal setting. Ask your partners what they think could have gone better. In asking for input without pointing fingers, you will strengthen trust in your facility, instead of creating an atmosphere where staff in your prison or jail feel defensive. If you have the opportunity to brief your command staff about your own findings, do so.

The most important point to this exercise is that you will have a better chance to move forward from the outcome of any incident if you treat that incident with some scientific distance, knowing full well that you have learned something from it.

Finally, move on! You will have plenty of opportunities in your career to try something differently. You will also have plenty of opportunities to learn from your mistakes without the useless exercise of pointing fingers.

Running Central Control for the fifth 12-hour shift in a row, an officer got the call to open a cell door in a housing unit with inmates from several different classifications. The cell he was called upon to open housed a medium-security inmate who could be escorted out of the housing unit with one escort officer. The escort officer who called Control had initiated his radio microphone after he started speaking and cut himself off.

The control officer heard a different cell number than what the escort officer said on the radio and opened a different cell door. This cell housed a maximum-security inmate who was also a mental health patient and prone to violence. He was only to come out of his cell in handcuffs and with two officers present. Yet here he was, out of his cell, surprised and staring at the escort officer.

The escort officer ordered the inmate back in his cell and the inmate followed the order. The control officer saw what had happened and closed the door. No harm, no foul. The officers finished their shift and had a laugh about the close call in the locker room.

Dodging a bullet

How many times have you written an incident report, shaking your head and counting your lucky stars that a series of missteps did not lead to one of your partners getting hurt, or an outcome in your facility that would end up in the news? How many times have you breathed a sigh of relief after seeing your career flash before your eyes because something pretty bad *almost* happened?

In the Corrections world, new policies, improved best practices and case law are generally changed after bad outcomes. When someone gets hurt, an agency is sued, or an inmate escapes, the response is often swift and the changes dramatic. Corrections staff are fired and policies picked apart.

When a bad set of circumstances does not create a bad outcome however, we laugh in relief and shake our head. Maybe we give the officer who almost lost their job some tough love and let them know, "You just dodged a bullet."

What we generally **do _not_ do** is tell anyone in authority about the incident. We don't want to get a partner in trouble for a mistake that didn't cause any issues, right? So, what happens the next time one of your partners makes the same mistake and something bad does happen? Could an institution avoid that injury, that lawsuit, or that riot with some risk management?

Near misses and close calls

In 1976, NASA established the Aviation Safety Reporting System (ASRS) with the mission of improving safety. The program serves commercial aviation, as well as government agencies involved in flying. This reporting system encourages pilots, air traffic controllers and others involved in the aviation world to submit reports when they see something that could potentially lead to a bad outcome. Two of the key components to the program's success are anonymity and limited immunity.

The program processed over 1.6 million reports by 2019 and produced over 60 safety studies.

In the manufacturing sector, risk management departments pay attention to near misses and close calls. There is a cultural expectation, which is spurred on by the certifications of factories, that when a mistake is made, the employees involved in the mistake will self-report to their factory floor managers. There is also an expectation that when a mistake is made, management will not punish an employee who self-reports an honest mistake or judgment call that could have ended badly.

<u>You are the risk manager</u>

If the control officer and escort officer were to sit down and seriously talk about what went wrong in the scenario above, what would be the most effective way to dissect the close call and produce a lesson?

Starting with self-reflection always gives you credibility if you are going to generate a report about a close call. The control officer should have double-checked the classification of the inmate he was letting out of a cell; especially knowing he was dealing with a mixed-classification unit. The escort officer should speak more clearly when he uses his radio and make sure his entire transmission is broadcasting.

Telling someone else what you think they did wrong can be a little dicier. You must do it without attacking character. For example, the control officer can tell the escort officer that the escort officer is keying his mic after he starts speaking. He shouldn't tell the escort officer that no one can understand anything he says on the radio. As the receiver of constructive criticism, you will get more honesty if you invite and appreciate the criticism, knowing you will improve based on the useful information. Constructive criticism is a powerful communication tool for a team, but it takes a lot of trust between team members to give and receive criticism. On the giving side, trusting that the receiver won't blow up and shut down when hearing criticism. On the receiving side, knowing that your teammate is on your side when s/he gives you criticism.

Once you find out what you can personally improve to avoid a tragedy down the road, start looking for how a policy or procedure can help. Perhaps in a mixed housing unit, any movement should start with two officers. In some cases, it is much safer to open cell doors within the unit instead of from Central control. A good risk manager may find that working a Corrections officer 60 hours a week will cost more in liability than it saves in paying staff enough to attract a full roster.

When you come up with as much information as you can and find possible solutions to avoid a bad result in the future, put together a report to send up the chain of command. A good commander will be thrilled to have the information if it is presented with integrity.

Improving policies, best practices and procedures before disaster strikes in your correctional facility will save you and your team a lot of grief down the road. Reporting and dissecting close calls is an investment that will improve correctional officer safety while decreasing correctional facility liability. Having an effective safety reporting system in place will save the controlling agency the most liability by illustrating that decision-makers are actively seeking improvements in safety before critical incidents have a chance to cause any damage.

CHAPTER EIGHTEEN – The Care Component

Anyone who has seen their career flash before their eyes as a result of the following scenario will tell you it just took one quick thoughtless comment to change everything. S/he will also tell you some of the most caring and strong-willed Corrections professionals have found themselves in a similar predicament. This is because we work long hours with periods of minimal recovery. The strong character traits Corrections staff members are hired for can be diminished when we don't take care of ourselves. Patience, emotional intelligence and problem solving are perishable skills, especially when tested daily.

You've been running Control for the past ten hours, with two more to go. Inmate Smith is a mental health patient. Smith started early today, about 25 minutes into your shift and the guy is persistent. First, he asked for the nurse, stating he didn't feel good. Nurses are busy and overworked, you told him to submit a med slip. Smith contacted you no less than 15 times within two hours to tell you about all the ways he was not feeling well. You started with patience, but there was a lot going on and, at some point, you ignored Smith. He must have fallen asleep and stopped bothering you. Before he did, he told you he couldn't breathe and needed medical "right away!" You shook your head and told him "No one cares"," and the nurse is busy. You got a couple chuckles from a coworker.

That was a couple hours ago. Now, you hear a call over the radio for a medical emergency from Smith's housing unit. Much later, and well past shift change, after getting interviewed by District Attorney investigators and writing your report, you go home with the death of an inmate on your mind and what you could have done to prevent the death. Terms like "Federal Case" and "Deliberate Indifference" are floating around. You have been directed by your union rep to "call this number" for an attorney.

There are at least three major components at play in the very real above scenario; Finite resources, tested patience and reduced empathy. Each of these components exist on a sliding scale within every Corrections facility and among each staff member.

Finite resources

Corrections nurses and sworn staff are far outnumbered by the people who regularly call for help. There is a constant triage taking place in a custody setting. Everchanging circumstances keep staff figuring and refiguring where their efforts are needed and in what order to handle emergencies. To exacerbate this issue further, most of our jails nationwide are operating grossly short-staffed today, some missing two or three shifts worth of personnel.

When an inmate repeatedly believes s/he is having an emergency or is seeking attention or obviously faking a medical issue to manipulate staff, it will be natural for staff to prioritize other inmate medical calls before coming back to the repeat faker. Care and custody have to apply to the entire inmate population and sometimes what would normally be Priority-One will move to third or fourth in line if there is a probability that the emergent needs of other inmates are more apparent.

Your patience meter

We are only human and after a constant barrage of false alarms and imagined emergencies, even the most patient Control officer may lose his edge. With many other calls to navigate and safety measures to keep in place, staff members will meter out how much effort they will give one inmate at any given time. If you had one staff member for every inmate in your facility, you could spend the entire day getting to the bottom of why Inmate Smith thinks he may have a medical emergency.

Maybe he's bored, maybe he is mortified by the voices in his head. Maybe he is actually, just this once, having a medical emergency. Smith, however, is one of several inmates at any given time who is testing your patience. It takes a lot of internal fortitude to maintain that patience meter as more tests pile on from different directions.

Reduced empathy

This is the component most likely to land you in federal court, because it directly relates to the term "Deliberate Indifference." It is also related to a defense mechanism Corrections professionals employ to protect our psyche. If we showed full empathy for every emotional input we receive from inmates, whether real or fabricated to manipulate staff, we would not survive the correctional environment. We therefore distance ourselves within our interactions with inmates. We do so just enough to remain protected, but still actually care about the outcome of any situation and show it, bearing in mind the mission of care and custody. So far, so good.

Things get dicey when a Corrections professional, exhausted by years of sustained overtime, exhibits false bravado and falls into the easy culture of carelessness, like nothing bothers him. He shows off for his colleagues and for some of the more sophisticated inmates who also exhibit indifference to protect their own psyche. The staff member starts walking and speaking like he doesn't have a care at all. Then, an inmate says something or does something any professional *should* care about and the staffer's response, "I don't care" becomes a headline in the local paper.

Control what you can

Staffing shortages are a larger issue than any one Corrections Officer. Additionally, your patience meter will fluctuate and take more hits when staffing is low. More sleep, exercise and a developed sense of humor will improve your resiliency. You can feed your patience meter to an extent. I believe this is easier said than done, considering the past two years in Corrections, but it's not impossible.

What you can absolutely control every shift is how much care you express in your duties towards the people in your custody. Not to be confused with weakness, high levels of care do not translate to less accountability. You can expect good behavior from inmates while simultaneously showing a professional level of care that will keep you legally safer.

Care will also protect your own psyche as much as emotional distance will. The two can exist in tandem and should. In the case of a possibly imaginary or faked medical emergency, play it safe and treat the event like a training exercise if it helps you focus on making the right moves. An inmate who has already been seen several times by the nurse and just won't quit calling for help may need to be moved to a location with more direct observation if you can justify the move within your policy.

The Control Operator may not be required to verbally engage with this inmate in order to act, but if you choose to connect via intercom with a difficult inmate, you will need to remain neutral or show some level of care. If you protect your frustrations with a careless remark, your intentions will be questioned despite your best efforts and any bad outcome will be amplified by the comments you make as you carry out your duties.

Shooting for the Moon

When NASA landed a manned spacecraft on the moon in 1969, they did not just fire the rocket and land it in one shot. With some definite calculations, science, and lessons from past mistakes, NASA pointed the spacecraft at the moon, knowing the astronauts would need to make some adjustments along the way. There was no one singular perfect path to the landing.

Navigating a career in Corrections and making it to retirement unharmed is a difficult task. The points, lessons and advice in this book are much easier to read and write about than to put into practice. It takes constant adjustments, regular reflection, and periodic reminders to stay on course.

You will make mistakes.

Your character skills will strengthen and weaken on sliding scales, affected by the amount of sleep you have, the number of overtime hours you've worked, your personal relationships, the health of your cat.

You will lose your yoga calm from time to time. You will make bad judgement calls.

Move forward and do not be defined by your mistakes. Learn from them and keep your mission in mind. Lean on your partners. Trust them to call you out when you need to make an adjustment.

Pushing yourself every day to do just a little better and to be mindful of your interactions with others will keep your mind sharp and your attitude positive.

You will have good days in Corrections, and you will have some terrible moments. You will also often win a verbal judo match with an inmate. The inmate may even thank you at the end of an exchange. That's a win.

Likewise, you will see an interaction fall apart in real time and you will have to go hands-on. Stay on task and control the threat. Nothing more, nothing less. Do not intend on proving your power, use all the back-up you have to control a threat without harming your own people, or the person who causes the threat.

With clear intention of doing no harm in all your interactions, of being a guardian, you will stand a much better chance of keeping your psyche healthy throughout your career and your career legally unharmed. Maintaining your mental health will keep your personal relationships intact and give you a better chance at a long and healthy retirement once you have finished serving your community.

Made in the USA
Middletown, DE
22 October 2022

13291738R00088